THE LAYMAN'S BIBLE COMMENTARY

THE LAYMAN'S BIBLE COMMENTARY
IN TWENTY-FIVE VOLUMES

THE LAYMAN'S
BIBLE COMMENTARY

Balmer H. Kelly, *Editor*

Donald G. Miller   *Associate Editors*   Arnold B. Rhodes

Dwight M. Chalmers, *Editor, John Knox Press*

VOLUME 8

THE BOOK OF
EZRA

THE BOOK OF
NEHEMIAH

THE BOOK OF
ESTHER

THE BOOK OF
JOB

Balmer H. Kelly

JOHN KNOX PRESS
RICHMOND, VIRGINIA

© M. E. Bratcher 1962

All rights reserved. No part of this book may be reproduced in any manner whatsoever without written permission except in the case of brief quotations embodied in critical articles and reviews. For information address John Knox Press, Richmond, Virginia 23209.

Published in Great Britain by SCM Press Ltd., London. Published simultaneously in Canada by The Ryerson Press, Toronto.

Fourth printing 1971

International Standard Book Number: 0-8042-3008-0
Library of Congress Catalog Card Number: 59-10454
Printed in the United States of America

PREFACE

The LAYMAN'S BIBLE COMMENTARY is based on the conviction that the Bible has the Word of good news for the whole world. The Bible is not the property of a special group. It is not even the property and concern of the Church alone. It is given to the Church for its own life but also to bring God's offer of life to all mankind —wherever there are ears to hear and hearts to respond.

It is this point of view which binds the separate parts of the LAYMAN'S BIBLE COMMENTARY into a unity. There are many volumes and many writers, coming from varied backgrounds, as is the case with the Bible itself. But also as with the Bible there is a unity of purpose and of faith. The purpose is to clarify the situations and language of the Bible that it may be more and more fully understood. The faith is that in the Bible there is essentially one Word, one message of salvation, one gospel.

The LAYMAN'S BIBLE COMMENTARY is designed to be a concise non-technical guide for the layman in personal study of his own Bible. Therefore, no biblical text is printed along with the comment upon it. This commentary will have done its work precisely to the degree in which it moves its readers to take up the Bible for themselves.

The writers have used the Revised Standard Version of the Bible as their basic text. Occasionally they have differed from this translation. Where this is the case they have given their reasons. In the main, no attempt has been made either to justify the wording of the Revised Standard Version or to compare it with other translations.

The objective in this commentary is to provide the most helpful explanation of fundamental matters in simple, up-to-date terms. Exhaustive treatment of subjects has not been undertaken.

In our age knowledge of the Bible is perilously low. At the same time there are signs that many people are longing for help in getting such knowledge. Knowledge of and about the Bible is, of course, not enough. The grace of God and the work of the Holy Spirit are essential to the renewal of life through the Scriptures. It is in the happy confidence that the great hunger for the Word is a sign of God's grace already operating within men, and that the Spirit works most wonderfully where the Word is familiarly known, that this commentary has been written and published.

THE EDITORS AND
THE PUBLISHERS

THE BOOKS OF
EZRA AND NEHEMIAH

INTRODUCTION

Composition

In the Bibles used in Protestant churches there stand side by side two books, corresponding in name to two great figures of Jewish history, Ezra and Nehemiah. The undoubted prominence and importance of each in the period when the Jews were being restored to the Promised Land is fittingly symbolized by this device, but it obscures the fact that quite probably the two men were contemporary and the more important fact that undoubtedly the two "books" were originally one integrated history. That this is true is indicated by the subject matter as well as by the way in which the ancient scribes, the Masoretes, identified the work.

It is apparent also that the Ezra-Nehemiah story was connected originally with the larger body of literary material we now know as First and Second Chronicles. A comparison of II Chronicles 36:22-23 with Ezra 1:1-4 shows the chronological connection between the two and suggests that in an original form First and Second Chronicles, Ezra, and Nehemiah were combined in a single history with perhaps fewer historical difficulties than are posed by the present arrangement and contents of the separate works.

For, as simple and direct as much of the present edition of Ezra and Nehemiah is, there are problems of background and relationship which as yet have no definitive solution. One of these is occasioned by the existence of a version of the same material, in somewhat different arrangement, including some additional matters and diverging in some details from the Books of Ezra and Nehemiah as we have them. This is the "Greek Ezra," a work which many regard as a better rendering of the original work than the form found in the Hebrew Bible and in the English versions. The relationship between the Hebrew books and this Greek work, still further complicated by confusing nomenclature, can be traced in a Bible dictionary.

Of more direct importance in the study of Ezra and Nehemiah is an understanding of the various sources used by the compiler of this history. Here again there are problems, but there are also some definite conclusions based upon clear evidence available to the reader of the books. To begin with, a glance at the marginal note at Ezra 4:7 will indicate that a long section, 4:8—6:18, is not in the Hebrew language but in Aramaic. A look at this section, moreover, will reveal the fact that most of it is concerned with official correspondence. Although the English version does not indicate it, another shorter section, 7:12-26, also official correspondence, is similarly in Aramaic rather than Hebrew. The presence of these two sections written in one of the official languages of the Persian period, along with their appropriate contents, suggests immediately that here the compiler of the history relied on actual copies of the original, simply transcribing them for his own work.

In addition to these obvious sources there are other more subtle but quite definite indications that the "author" of the work was a "compiler"—in fact, surely the same as the author-compiler of the Books of Chronicles. We find reference to "the book of the genealogy of those who came up at the first," followed by a direct quotation from such a book (Neh. 7:5 and 7:6-73a) and reference to "the Book of the Chronicles" (Neh. 12:23).

At the base of the present work, moreover, there was probably an original, firsthand report by Ezra himself, of which some of the narrative phrased in the first person is a remainder. Certainly in the present work, although possibly not so placed by the original compiler, is the firsthand, definitely autobiographical report of Nehemiah, commonly called the Nehemiah Memoir and including Nehemiah 1-7 and scattered portions elsewhere in the book.

Historical Setting

The mention of problems prepares the way for the major problem faced by anyone who attempts to get a completely clear and satisfactory historical picture of the Ezra-Nehemiah material. As in the case of the other problems, there is much that is clear, but some puzzling details and one great uncertainty remain. The uncertainty is the relationship between the two men and their historical order.

It appears at first glance that the situation is unconfused. Ezra is dated in his volume (Ezra 7:7) as having returned to Jerusalem in "the seventh year of Ar-ta-xerxes the king." If we assume that Artaxerxes I is meant, as seems likely, then Ezra would be placed in Jerusalem from 458 B.C. onward. Nehemiah worked in Jerusalem from "the twentieth year of King Ar-ta-xerxes" (Neh. 2:1) to sometime after "the thirty-second year of Ar-ta-xerxes" (Neh. 13:6), or between 445 and 438 B.C. The main difficulty with such a seemingly simple chronological arrangement is to be found in the story the books themselves tell. Ezra is clearly represented as having come to Jerusalem with the intent of teaching the Law (Ezra 7:10) and, in fact, as charged with the responsibility of enforcing the Jewish Law (Ezra 7:25-26). It is not, however, until after the arrival of Nehemiah, thirteen years later, that the story records Ezra's reading of the Law (Neh. 8:1-8). Although the latter account could refer to a repetition of an earlier ceremony, it is strange that such a ceremony should have gone unrecorded. The difficulty, moreover, is compounded when we realize that if the present arrangement is correct, then we must assume that the reforms Ezra is described as having initiated (Ezra 9-10) had to be reinstituted thirteen years later by Nehemiah (Neh. 13).

Because of this, along with other minor details which conflict with the present order, some interpreters take the date of Ezra's arrival as referring to the reign of Artaxerxes II, that is, to 398 B.C. Although such a view does fit some features of the book better than any other, it runs into another difficulty in that it requires too late a date for the compilation of the book.

Still another view makes Ezra and Nehemiah contemporaries in Jerusalem, as does the traditional view, but reverses the traditional order of their coming. In this view it becomes necessary, of course, to change the date of Ezra's arrival, a common suggestion being to substitute "the thirty-seventh year" for "the seventh year" (the error would be explainable on the basis of the Hebrew text). Although this does not by any means solve all of the difficulties of the text, it does make for a reasonably consistent and coherent picture.

When it is asked how the present arrangement came about if the order of the men is to be reversed, we must assume that the fundamental difficulty lay in the placing of the large part of the Nehemiah Memoir (Neh. 1-7). That this is not entirely a guess is indicated by the Greek Ezra, which does not include Nehemiah 1-7 in its present position, but connects Nehemiah 7:73b to the end of the Book of Ezra. It is possible that these chapters were wrongly placed in the Ezra narrative, conceivably because the reference to Nehemiah in 8:9 made it advisable to explain his presence in Jerusalem.

The most that can be said is that although the Books of Ezra and Nehemiah are historically valuable for the features of the period of the restoration of the Jewish people to their homeland, and although they are accurate in matters of detail, the chronological order they present is extremely uncertain.

The Message

The uncertainty of chronology should be no matter of great concern, for as in the case of the other historical writings of the Bible, the purpose of the Books of Ezra and Nehemiah is not to give us a step-by-step account of events. Nor does their importance for us rest on their exact recital of chronological fact. They are documents which above all express faith, and do so in such a fashion as to support faith, just as do the earlier books of Israel's history.

There is, in fact, a close similarity between the Books of Ezra and Nehemiah and the record of the Exodus events. Like the earlier record, these books recite the great redemptive act of God who himself initiates and carries forward the return of the Chosen People. God, not Ezra or Nehemiah, and especially not Darius or Artaxerxes, is the great Actor in this account. His word is the efficient power and his will directs the course of events. As before, his grace calls his Elect People from bondage and leads them through the perils of the wilderness and into the Land of Promise, where his grace does not desert them. In its rehearsal of this work of God's grace the story of Ezra and Nehemiah holds forth for God's people in succeeding days the assurance of the power of the unchanging word and grace of God.

These books, then, put together the fact of God's continuing activity for his people and the fact of their obedience, never perfect but there all the same. God was beginning again with his own; they were beginning again in honest attempt to understand

and do the will of God. The Church will do well to listen to these records as the Word of God to her own life, and to hear from them the possibilities for her own renewal under God.

OUTLINE

The Return Under Sheshbazzar. Ezra 1:1—2:70

The Decree (1:1-4)
The Response (1:5-11)
The Lists of Returning Jews (2:1-70)

The Construction of the Temple. Ezra 3:1—6:22

Early Efforts (3:1-13)
The Samaritan Conflict (4:1—6:22)

The Return Under Ezra. Ezra 7:1—10:44

The Permission to Return (7:1-28)
Ezra's Return (8:1-36)
Religious Reforms (9:1—10:44)

Nehemiah's Visit to Jerusalem. Nehemiah 1:1—7:73a

Background (1:1—2:20)
The Work on the Wall (3:1-32)
Opposition (4:1-23)
Administrative Difficulties (5:1-19)
The Completion of the Wall (6:1—7:4)
Genealogical List (7:5-73a)

Religious Reformation. Nehemiah 7:73b—10:39

The Reading of the Law (7:73b—8:12)
The Observance of the Feast of Tabernacles (8:13-18)
The Firm Covenant (9:1—10:39)

Aspects of the New Community. Nehemiah 11:1—13:3

Lists (11:1—12:26)
The Dedication of the Wall (12:27-43)
The Worship in the Temple (12:44—13:3)

Nehemiah's Second Visit to Jerusalem. Nehemiah 13:4-31

COMMENTARY

THE RETURN UNDER SHESHBAZZAR

Ezra 1:1—2:70

The Decree (1:1-4)

Already in the first chapter there appear clearly the themes which will mark the entire history of the Ezra-Nehemiah books, and which make this history, for all its multiple details and prosaic character, great religious writing. From the beginning the whole is set against the background of a mighty act of God, which is the working out of his creative and efficient word. Historically the date is the "first year of Cyrus king of Persia," that is, the first year when he became king of Babylon (538 B.C.); and the occasion is the pronouncement of a decree of this king, encouraging the Jewish exiles to return to the land from which they had been driven by Nebuchadnezzar a half century before. But historical date and political occasion are secondary to the important fact that behind the king's action was the activity of God himself, who "stirred up the spirit of Cyrus." Thus the occasion was a time of fulfillment and accomplishment. The word of God spoken through Jeremiah long ago was now becoming a full deed; the promise of ultimate return from exile was becoming a saving fact. Although the name of the king of Persia stands at the head of the story, we do not read far before we discover that the real actor is not Cyrus but the Lord. Similarly we soon come to understand that the event which is to be described in this historical book is not simply a happening in a great empire, nor even the beginning again of a nation, significant as these are in themselves, but this is a new *exodus*, an event worthy to be placed alongside that earlier memorable event as a testimony to the saving power of God and to his Covenant fidelity to his people.

The decree (vss. 2-4) has certain parallels to other proclamations and inscriptions of the time, and there is nothing in it to suggest that it does not represent substantially the sense of the actual proclamation by Cyrus. It is repeated in 6:3-5 in different form, but this may reflect the difference between original oral and written forms.

It is known from contemporary sources outside the Bible that Cyrus showed interest in the various deities worshiped in his empire. His acknowledgment that "the LORD" had given him victory over all the kingdoms of the earth is not to be understood as the confession of saving faith, for it is later balanced by the expression "may his God be with him" (vs. 3), which indicates that he actually regarded each god as local and national.

Another dominant motif of the entire Ezra-Nehemiah story appears in the reference to "the house of the LORD," which is to be rebuilt. Thus, at the center of the undertaking of the returning Jewish exiles there was to be placed, not a national recrudescence or a restoration of a ruined city, but a religious revival, symbolized always by the rebuilding of the Temple.

The decree, moreover, represents the undertaking as one in which the entire exilic community is to join. Not only will there be some who return ("each survivor"), but those who choose to remain in Babylon will give the material assistance which the returnees will need, and especially will contribute to the central business of rebuilding the house of God (vs. 4).

The Response (1:5-11)

The constitution of the community of restoration is indicated when the response to the proclamation is described among the Jewish leaders in Babylon. These are specified as the family heads of the tribes of "Judah and Benjamin" and "the priests and the Levites." Thus, essentially, the undertaking is interpreted as one that centers in the Davidic tribes and in those persons associated with the worship of the Temple. The decree itself, of course, made no such limitations, but the story does, and the actual endeavor probably did. Thus again it is emphasized that this is a new and a *true* beginning, an act of God to which the people respond, and those who represent the ancient Messianic hope and the religious faith of the nation are especially designated as the ones who hear and obey the word of promise as it is fulfilled.

In harmony with the original decree, which had stipulated that the returning Jews were to be aided by others (1:4), the account of the response among the exiles includes not only the decision of some but the help which others gave in money and goods (1:6; compare Exod. 3:22). The last part of verse 6 is difficult, but it may refer to the extraordinary volume of gifts.

Paralleling the general support, the king also further encourages the returnees by placing in the charge of their leader "the vessels of the house of the LORD which Nebuchadnezzar had carried away from Jerusalem." The following detailed list is extremely uncertain, as the marginal notes indicate. The exact meaning of some of the names of the vessels escapes us. In the original Hebrew text, moreover, the numbers of the separate items and the total do not agree. The Revised Standard Version has utilized the alternate numbering found in the Greek Bible (see also the list of objects taken from the Temple, in II Kings 25:13-17).

The undertaking is described as having been committed by Cyrus to one "Shesh-bazzar the prince of Judah" (vs. 8). In view of the fact that such a person plays no further part in the story (but see 5:16), and that on the contrary the figure of Zerubbabel assumes greater and greater importance (2:2; 3:2, 8; 4:3; 5:2; see also Haggai 1:1; Zech. 4:6-10), it appears that Sheshbazzar was influential only in the very early stages of the return. On the other hand, it is possible that either the historian confused the two and thought of them as one, or that they were actually two names for one man (see, for example, Dan. 1:6-7, although "Shesh-bazzar" and "Zerubbabel" are both Babylonian in form).

The Lists of Returning Jews (2:1-70)

The first of a number of lists added to the story is made up of men who were apparently leaders. (The Greek version calls them "guides.") The same list occurs with a few variations and with one more name in Nehemiah 7:7. The probability is that the original list contained twelve names (as in Nehemiah), thus preserving the pattern of the twelve tribes of the original Exodus and of the first settlement of the land (see also the selection of twelve disciples by Jesus).

The major list of returnees occurs in verses 2b-35. The numbers again, as is often the case with the Ezra material, are uncertain and vary considerably between the Greek version and the Hebrew, and also in the similar lists in Nehemiah 7. The variations suggest errors of copying from the official lists of the Persian Empire which must have been used in the compilation of this history. A Bible dictionary will give the derivation of the various names, which are not arranged by type of name but fall into two large classifications: those named by family group (2b-20) and those named by city (21-35).

At verse 36 another list begins, covering Temple personnel, naming first of all certain "priests" (vss. 36-39), then "Levites," who at this time were regarded as Temple servants and apparently were mainly unwilling to return (vs. 40; see also 8:15-20), then "singers" (vs. 41), then porters (vs. 42), then other Temple servants (vss. 43-54), and finally "the sons of Solomon's servants," apparently an ancient class among the larger group of servants (vss. 55-58).

The next list is made up of those whose genealogy was uncertain. These took part in the return, although possibly not in a fully accredited status. In this brief list there appears the note of deep concern for racial and religious purity which became later so pronounced an aspect of the whole period of the restoration. It cannot be doubted that one factor that helped strengthen the sense of exclusiveness that came to mark the Jewish people was this very preparation for return and the rigid search for bona fide Jewish exiles among the empire lists of Persia. The "Urim and Thummim" represent the sacred lot, although there is no evidence that such a device was used in the Temple that was built by these returned exiles (see I Sam. 14:41).

The lists close with a group of summaries, again disagreeing in the various versions as to the exact numbers. The expression "they came to the house of the LORD" in verse 68 refers to the site of the Temple, or the verse may be misplaced, as some interpreters believe.

Verse 70 closes the list and the account of the initial stages of the return with a kind of idealized summary, suggesting that the new conquest of the land is complete.

THE CONSTRUCTION OF THE TEMPLE

Ezra 3:1—6:22

Early Efforts (3:1-13)

As would be expected, the first efforts at reconstruction of a regular worship in Jerusalem had to do with the construction of an altar. The work is represented as having begun in "the seventh month," although it is not clear precisely what the original point of reference in the date is. In earlier times the altar had been used independently of the Temple, and so it was now (see II Sam. 24:25).

The leaders are identified as "Jeshua" (Joshua) the high priest (see Haggai 1:1, 12, 14; 2:2; Zech. 3:1-10) and "Zerubbabel." The chronology is by no means certain, for both Haggai and Zechariah seem to suggest that the work here described went on at a later date (during the reign of Darius). The construction of the altar according to the specifications in the Law of Moses (note again the strong sense of continuity with the past) is described as having been accomplished (quickly?) because "fear was upon them because of the peoples of the lands [neighboring countries or aliens settled in Palestine]" (vs. 3). Whether this means that the Jews feared that these people would bring informing action against them to Persia, or whether they naturally desired the help of God in their new and critical situation, is not clear. At any rate, they felt that a rapid reinstitution of the sacrifice ritual was necessary. It is described, moreover, as having incorporated from the beginning the characteristic which it later had, that of continual sacrifice, morning and evening.

Along with the reinstitution of the sacrifice went an observance of the Feast of Tabernacles, traditionally the most joyful of the feasts of the Israelite calendar. Since it was also traditionally the celebration of the wilderness life of Israel, it made a fitting commemoration of the new exodus and the new settlement of the land.

The third step was the beginning of construction of the Temple itself, although probably not much work was accomplished at first. The story is told with overtones reminiscent of the building of the great Temple of Solomon (see I Kings 5). The description also indicates something of the magnitude of the task, since such expensive materials would have to be brought from faraway places.

The chapter closes with an account of the mingled joy and weeping which attended the actual laying of the foundation. There were those whose eyes were turned backward and who wept because they remembered, or had heard of, the former magnificence of the Temple. Although this new Temple would not compare with the Solomonic Temple, certainly not in this preliminary stage, the beginning of work on it represented real sacrifice on the part of the people, and its completion in a time of poverty would represent greater dedication than did the former Temple. That it was started at all is a credit to the faith and loyalty of the returning Jews and to the loyal love of God, whose power and mighty acts were celebrated in the antiphonal song sung on the occasion. The translation of verse 9 is awkward, and the name "Judah" does not belong here (see Neh. 7:43).

The Samaritan Conflict (4:1—6:22)

The Samaritan Offer (4:1-5)

The beginning described in such optimistic terms in chapter 3 was just that, a beginning. For the completion of the undertaking it was necessary to wait some twenty years. Opposition on the part of native dwellers in Palestine certainly was a prime factor in the delay (see 3:3). These "adversaries of Judah and Benjamin" were the descendants of peoples of mixed stock who had been brought in by the conquerors of Israel in the late eighth or early seventh century. They appealed to the Jews on the basis of a common religion. The abrupt refusal of Zerubbabel, Jeshua, and the other leaders is a reminder again of the exclusivism which grew rapidly during this period. At the same time it is a reminder that the Samaritans did not represent a pure tradition of Covenant loyalty or even of monotheistic worship (see II Kings 17:29-34). A co-operative venture at this time might seem to have been wise and tolerant in the light of the difficulties which the returning exiles faced. But at the price of compromise it would have been fatal.

The true motives which led the Samaritans to make the offer of help are now revealed as, using every possible means, they undertake to discourage and even thwart the Jews in the task of building. The extent of this opposition is summarized by the editor as having stretched from the days of Cyrus to the reign of Darius.

Typical Opposition (4:6-24)

In the following section the historian apparently used an Aramaic document which included correspondence growing out of the kind of opposition he had just dealt with. It is likely that most of the material did not come from the time he is recounting; in fact, it is otherwise dated. Rather the editor must have used it with little concern for historical and chronological exactitude, because he felt that it typified the adversities facing the Jews.

"Ahasuerus" in verse 6 is generally identified as Xerxes, who reigned after Darius. As indicated above, then, the reference is out of historical order, or it is possible that the editor wished to indicate in this fashion that the opposition he is chronicling continued long after the time with which he is specifically concerned.

The letter to Artaxerxes is similarly out of chronological order, but may have been used as an illustration of the historian's point. The language shifts from Hebrew to Aramaic at 4:8, continuing to 6:18. Verses 7 and 8 suggest the possibility that in the original source there were two letters, one from "Mithredath and Tabeel" ("Bishlam" could be a greeting), the other from "Rehum" and "Shimshai"; the two letters would have been combined by the historian, who included two introductions (see also vss. 8-11). The list in verse 9 is a reminder of the extensive political machinery of the Persian Empire and of the fact that along with the native Samaritan opposition there was hostility on the part of the officials. "Osnappar" is a variant form of "Ashurbanipal," the Assyrian king. "The River" is, of course, the Euphrates.

The clear reference of the letters is to the "walls" and "foundations" of the city rather than the Temple. It reflects a time later than the first years of the Return. The officials see the threat posed by the Jews as essentially political and economic. They fear that the strengthening nation will come to the point where it will pay neither "tribute" nor tax ("custom") and will not submit to the forced labor and military drafts which were the custom of the day. The translation of the last part of verse 13 is a guess.

In the letter of Artaxerxes the appeal of the officials is answered in the affirmative. The records were consulted, and they showed that Jerusalem was indeed, as charged, rebellious to empire ambitions. Therefore it was ordered that the "city be not rebuilt." This cessation the historian now identifies as the reason why the work on the Temple ceased.

Resumption of Work on the Temple (5:1—6:22)

Here we are once again in the reign of Darius (as at 4:5). The story reopens with "the house of God which is in Jerusalem" and is concerned with the efforts of Zerubbabel and Jeshua to rebuild. Having been frustrated in the first attempt (by the Samaritans), and having turned in the meantime to other pressing concerns, the Jews were slow to resume work on the Temple. The preaching of Haggai and Zechariah, however, bore fruit and led to a renewed effort on the part of leaders and people. Zechariah, who is here designated "the son of Iddo," is called in his own prophecy "the son of Berechiah, son of Iddo." We know that there was a "prophet Iddo" (II Chron. 13:22), and it is possible that his name became attached to the entire genealogy of his descendants.

Although verse 2, taken alone, sounds as if the historian thought of this effort as the initial work on the Temple, verse 16 makes it clear that this was not the case, for there Sheshbazzar and his work are mentioned. The help of the prophets to which reference is made is probably the encouragement they offered (for example, Haggai 2:1-9; Zech. 3:1-10).

Once again opposition developed, a reminder of the prospects that must be faced when men set themselves to do the will of God. This time it is the officials of the Persian satrapy: Tattenai, the "governor" (probably a subordinate rather than the highest official), and Shethar-bozenai, probably a scribe.

The Letter of Tattenai (5:6-17)

The historian again breaks into the story to incorporate material from the collection of correspondence he was using. The term "the governors" in verse 6 is uncertain. Some translations and interpreters treat it as a proper name ("the Apharsachites"), but most regard it as a reference to a group of minor officials.

The letter gives in greater detail the reason for the Persian officials' concern. They have found in Jerusalem that work on the Temple is proceeding rapidly. The term "huge stones" probably refers to an unusual type of stone rather than to size; "timber" may be the beams which served as support for the roof.

Although in the historian's account the original question asked by the officials had been left unanswered (5:3-4), here the answer is given in full. It is interesting for a number of reasons but especially in that it identifies the reason for the Exile as infidelity on the part of the Jews. In verse 15 there is an apparent contradiction, assuming on the one hand the existence of a Temple in which the sacred objects could be stored and, on the other hand, recording the command that "the house of God be rebuilt on its site." Once again the original undertaking is associated with the name of Sheshbazzar (see 1:8), implying that he and Zerubbabel were different persons and that in the time of Cyrus an actual beginning was made in the work of rebuilding the Temple.

The Answer of Darius (6:1-12)

Ecbatana was the site of the summer palace of Cyrus, and here search was made. The original decree was found in the "archives," doubtless similar to repositories recently discovered in Persia.

Verses 3-5 are virtually the same as 5:13-15, at least close enough to indicate that they are both versions of the original document giving the actual form of Cyrus' decree. This would have been a document elaborating the simple permission to return (1:2-4) and may have included provisions for other like undertakings in the Persian Empire. The translation "and burnt offerings are brought" is probably in error; the original seems to indicate some further architectural expression, possibly a reference to the fashion in which the foundations were to be laid.

Only two dimensions are supplied, and these are at variance with the dimensions of Solomon's Temple, which was described as "sixty cubits long, twenty cubits wide, and thirty cubits high" (I Kings 6:2). These were also probably the specifications in Cyrus' decree. A "cubit" approximates the forearm length. The term "courses" refers to a section, or a series of rows of bricks or stones in the wall.

Verses 6-12 resume the matter which was raised by Tattenai. Darius expressed his intent to further the edict of Cyrus and, furthermore, charged the Persian officials to support the work. As an indication of his own support he directs that the undertaking be financed from the royal treasury. The prophecies of Haggai and Zechariah, contemporary to these events, do not encourage us to believe that such a grant was ever actually received, for the work seems to have been carried on at great sacrifice. The possibility is that although the grant was made—and historical records outside the Bible confirm similar grants—the officials simply did not carry out the direct charge of the king.

There is no reason to doubt the authenticity of the provision for regular financial support of the sacrificial worship in the restored Temple. It was quite in keeping with the practice of the Persian kings to make such provisions, possibly as political expedients and possibly as religious acts of appeasement (vs. 10). The fact that such support was not given may be explained again by the failure of subordinate officials to carry out the king's decree, or by the unwillingness of the Jewish community to utilize such help.

Verses 11 and 12 detail the punishment to be meted out to anyone altering the decree in word or practice. In verse 12 the term "name" is used in the sense of "person" or "self."

The Completion of the Temple (6:13-22)

The meaning of the historical events just recited is now apparent as the historian tells of the climax, when the Temple is finally completed. Against all opposition it is done. And it is done always by the power of God's command, which takes precedence over the political decrees of the Persian kings. This building stands completed as a witness to the power of God's word to perform the thing he purposes.

It is also a symbol for a new, restored, and re-created Israel. The twelve tribes are present at the rededication ceremonies, and the Temple stands at the center of their national life. The new beginning is, moreover, fittingly celebrated by a Passover observance, emphasizing the similarity between this new exodus and conquest of the land and the one centuries before. The new beginning includes a purification of the religious leaders (vs. 20) and a purification of the people themselves in the community which is made up of both returned exiles and the other dwellers in the land (vs. 21).

Over all there is sounded the constant note of "joy." It was more than a political celebration, more than a displaced person's gladness at his return home. This was a deeply religious joy, "for the LORD had made them joyful." It was a joy over the power of God's word, over the grace which gave them a new beginning, over the presence of the Lord in the Temple and community, and over the future blessing which awaited them as the people of the Covenant. In telling his story the historian let it be clear that the same joy awaits those who venture in faith in response to the word of God's promise.

The reference to "the king of Assyria" is, of course, out of place, unless "Assyria" be understood to mean "Persia." It should be noted also that the language shifts from Aramaic back to Hebrew after 6:18 (see 4:7-8).

THE RETURN UNDER EZRA

Ezra 7:1—10:44

The Permission to Return (7:1-28)

Ezra and His Company (7:1-10)

Over a century intervened between the time of the completion of the Temple, recorded in chapter 6, and the events which are taken up in chapter 7, a century which is passed over with the words, "after this." As in the case of the Pentateuchal narrative, this history is not concerned with giving a precise and full chronological account, but with chronicling "the mighty acts of God." The time is now the reign of Artaxerxes (see also 4:7). The main character of the new effort is introduced in customary fashion by a genealogy, tracing Ezra's line back to Aaron (although the genealogy, parallel to I Chronicles 6:3-15, is marked by several gaps). Ezra is named as a "scribe," a term which probably had original reference to some responsibility at the court of Persia. In the biblical account it is defined in reference to "the law of Moses." From the outset the importance of Ezra is fixed by three points: his place in the priesthood, his skill in the Law, and his piety ("for the hand of the LORD his God was upon him").

Although it is not specifically stated, it is apparent from the story that Ezra had asked for permission either to go to Jerusalem himself, or to lead a company there. The story opens with the king's permission (vs. 6) and continues with a brief list of the types of people who accompanied Ezra (vs. 7; see the list in 8:1-14). The vexing question of the date of Ezra's return (vss. 8-9) has been discussed in the Introduction. The exemplary character of Ezra is further stressed in verse 10.

The Letter of Artaxerxes (7:11-26)

Artaxerxes' letter of permission and charge to Ezra is given in Aramaic. Prominent features of this letter are its exaltation of Ezra, its insistence on "the law" (possibly one of the king's reasons for encouraging this return was a desire to stabilize a part of the empire), familiarity with Jewish religious practice (Ezra may have been the court "scribe" who wrote the decree), a direct demand of "the treasurers" that they give financial support to the

Temple worship, and exemption of Temple personnel from taxa-
tion. Most of the features were apparently normal procedure in
Persian court decrees.

Doxology (7:27-28)

For the first time Ezra is designated as the speaker, an indication that the source used by the historian here was a "memoir" of
Ezra himself. He speaks, appropriately, in a hymn of praise to
God for his work in moving the king to act, and for his mercies
to Ezra.

Ezra's Return (8:1-36)

As was the case with the earlier return (chs. 1-2), the account
of the return led by Ezra included a list of "the heads of their
fathers' houses" who accompanied him. The list testifies to the
strong feeling of solidarity with the past and to the equally strong
sense of racial and religious purity which marked the restoration
and later Judaism. The list corresponds in the main with the one
in chapter 2, so far as the family groups are concerned, although
there are minor differences.

The numbers total close to 1500 men, a sizable group, since
each would be accompanied by family and possibly some servants. This group, forming a caravan for travel, met by "the river
that runs to Ahava" (see also vs. 31), possibly one of the canals
near Babylon (see Ezek. 1:1). In the earlier return the Levites
were slack in responding; in the new venture no Levite appears
as the preparations are made for the journey. Verses 16-20 describe the way Ezra met the problem, and the success of his depu-
tation to "Iddo" at "Casiphia" (both otherwise unknown). Along
with the bare account of preparation goes the affirmation of faith
that all this was accomplished because of "the good hand of our
God upon us."

The same faith is particularly stressed in the account of the
fasting and prayer which were a prelude to the journey. Although
fasting was known in Israel from early times, it was in the last
centuries before Christ that it assumed its great importance for
Judaism, not only as a sign of repentance but especially as a central expression of faith and devotion to God.

With the mixture of hardheaded practicality and deep faith
which marks this entire literature, Ezra made special provision

for the safe arrival of the treasures which the caravan carried. The aggregate value of the silver seems abnormally high—the total worth would run into millions by modern standards—and it is probable that the figures have suffered in the transmission of the text. The community of Jews at Jerusalem did not in later years give evidence of having access to any such wealth.

The four months (see 8:31 and 7:8-9) required for the journey, which would have followed the normal trade route, indicate something of the difficulty such an undertaking involved. On arrival in Jerusalem there was a suitable rest period for the company. Then the completion of the journey was marked on the one hand by discharging the responsibilities carried with the treasures, and on the other by sacrifices which testified to the reunion of Israel (twelve for the twelve tribes) and to God's grace and blessing by which the journey had been begun and completed.

Religious Reforms (9:1—10:44)

The Problem and Ezra's Reaction (9:1-15)

On the occasion of the first exodus from Egypt, an event which colored the account and the fact of the return from Babylon, a primary reason for the failure of the people to live up to their Covenant responsibility was always seen to be their willingness to adopt the ways of Canaan and to combine elements of heathen religion with the worship of the Lord. The same threat appeared in the time of Ezra, and it was doubtless due to the stern measures he took that there grew up in Judaism at this time a strong sense of exclusivism, becoming in time the religious parochialism which marked the Pharisee of the New Testament.

The problem is described in 9:1-2, as reported to Ezra by leaders in the community. The list of "the peoples of the lands" is of course not meant to be an exact naming of contemporary peoples, for many of these had passed from the pages of history, but it is a historical reminder of the similar situation in the days of their ancestors (see parallel lists in Exod. 3:8; 13:5; Deut. 7:1; 20:17). The error was not that people engaged in mixed marriages as such, but that mixed marriages led to "abominations," that is, to corrupt and paganizing influences in religion and society.

Ezra's reaction was sharp and immediate. His classic gestures of mourning attracted a crowd who waited for his words. Here Ezra stands in the prophetic tradition, for the prophets before him had often engaged in similar dramatic and symbolic actions.

At the time of the evening sacrifice Ezra engaged in a public prayer which gave vivid expression to his own feelings and, appropriately for a leader of the community, served as a confession of corporate guilt. The prayer has some similarities to other great scriptural prayers (compare Neh. 9:6-37; Dan. 9:4-19) and combines confession and petition.

The prophetic view of history is implied in Ezra's confession, where the Exile is seen as the result of national sin rather than political events. Noticeable in the prayer also is the tenuous and brief beginning which the Return represents. Verse 9 is like the ancient confessions of Israel's faith which declared that once the people had been slaves in Egypt but were set free. Here again is the note of the new exodus.

Verses 10-12 introduce a series of commands which are said to have been given by "the prophets." As a matter of fact, the quotation fits Deuteronomy 7:1-3 better than any other passage, but is probably to be regarded as a general statement of the principles of religious purity inherent in all prophetic teaching. The specific matter of mixed marriage does appear in Malachi, also in the late period of Jewish history.

The prayer ends with a great confession of national sin and corporate guilt, the speaker identifying himself with the nation in its distress, as had Moses before him.

Public Confession and Covenant (10:1-5)

Ezra's example and prayer had immediate effect. Public repentance (vs. 1) is expressed by one Shecaniah, who proposes a drastic solution, namely, that the "foreign women" be "put away." This would probably mean exclusion from the community and certainly involved divorce or annulment. Shecaniah proposes this as "a covenant" with God, again a sign that underlying what appears to be a harsh measure was a sincere effort to fulfill the obligations which belonged to a Covenant people.

Ezra's Reform (10:6-17)

In line with Shecaniah's proposal there was held in Jerusalem a mass assembly, attendance at which was required under threat of severe penalties (vs. 8). The casual mention of "the heavy

rain" points to the inclement weather (December) and also to the
historical character of the narrative here. Although there was
some opposition to Ezra's proposed reform (vs. 15) the main
body of the people were in agreement, the only problem being
the practical method of determining the guilty without unduly
involving the time of the whole people. When such a solution was
presented (vs. 14), apparently the assembly was dismissed. Verses
16 and 17 detail the manner in which the designated officials
went about their work.

Record of Offenders (10:18-44)

The Book of Ezra closes with a list of those who "had married
foreign women" and who "put them away," making a sacrificial
offering for their guilt (see vs. 19). The list begins with priests
and includes in all slightly over 100 men (some of the figures are
not explicit).

Beyond any question the measures were harsh and contrast
with the spirit of such books as Ruth and Jonah. On the credit
side it must be said, however, that through such measures as these
the Jews were made more and more a people of the Law, a nation
centered especially in religious faith.

NEHEMIAH'S VISIT TO JERUSALEM
Nehemiah 1:1—7:73a

Background (1:1—2:20)

Nehemiah's Concern (1:1-11a)

As indicated in the Introduction, the material in the first part
of the Book of Nehemiah surely comes from an original memoir
kept by Nehemiah himself. The date with which the account
opens is either not a part of the original or is a mistake of the
editor in copying. The time of chapter 1 must be prior to the
events of chapter 2, which is dated in "the month of Nisan."
Chislev was the ninth month and Nisan the first in the Babylonian calendar. "The twentieth year" refers to the reign of
Artaxerxes I.

The story opens with the inquiry made by Nehemiah of a
group of travelers. Their report on the state of the people in "the
province" (Judea; see Ezra 2:1) tells of a shocking condition.

The city of Jerusalem especially is vulnerable to attack, since its walls are broken down and its gates breached. Although at first sight it might be supposed that the travelers refer to the results of the destruction wrought by Nebuchadnezzar's armies a century and a half before, careful consideration points to a more recent happening. Nehemiah's great anxiety certainly points to something relatively new. The likelihood is that Nehemiah, aware of the plans of the returned exiles, had expected to hear of a completed wall. It is also probable that the report given him referred to some such opposition as that specified in Ezra, chapter 4 (see comment).

Nehemiah's concern is expressed first in mourning and then in prayer (compare Ezra 9; Dan. 9:3-19). The prayer is largely built on phrases from Deuteronomy, which accounts for its similarities to the other prayers. It begins in confession as Nehemiah, like Ezra, identifies himself with the needy people. He appeals to God, remembering his promises of help, and he ends characteristically in self-dedication. It is no accident that Nehemiah's concern, expressed in prayer, led him straight to the point of personal commitment, for over and over in the Bible when an individual brings a real concern for others to God in prayer he finds that there comes to him an imperative call to serve in meeting those needs.

Nehemiah's Plan (1:11b—2:20)

Nehemiah's substantial position in the Persian court was that of "cupbearer." This was one of the most responsible of all court offices, and in a day when assassination was usually by poison the cupbearer was necessarily a loyal and respected person. It should be noted that as royal cupbearer Nehemiah was probably a eunuch. Many interpreters believe that Isaiah 56:3-5 is designed to give comfort to and to include in the religious community those who like Nehemiah might otherwise be excluded (Deut. 23:1).

The account of Nehemiah's request to Artaxerxes has the flavor of firsthand recollection (see especially Nehemiah's prayer between the king's question and his own response). No comment on the story is necessary, save to point out that the expression "the king's forest" refers to a royal preserve, probably in the mountains of Lebanon.

The account continues, undoubtedly based on Nehemiah's

memoirs, with the record of Nehemiah's journey to Jerusalem.
To be noted are the presence of an escort, which would give
Nehemiah status in his undertaking; his dealing with the pro-
vincial governors along the way; and especially the mention of
the two who will give Nehemiah such trouble later: Sanballat and
Tobiah. The former was probably a Samaritan leader (Beth-
horon was a town in Ephraim). Tobiah's designation as "the
servant" probably refers to some position he held in Persian pro-
vincial affairs.

At night, so as to avoid calling attention to his plan before it
was firm, and with only one mount, Nehemiah and a small company proceeded to a tour of inspection of the city walls. The
careful description again indicates that back of this record is a
journal kept by Nehemiah himself. The various place names are
difficult to identify, so that the actual course of the journey cannot now be traced with certainty. The "Jackal's Well" is more
literally "Dragon's Well" (probably En-rogel, beside which I
Kings 1:9 locates "the Serpent's Stone"). In verse 15 "the valley" is the valley of the Brook Kidron. The account reiterates in
verse 16 the secrecy of this initial inspection.

With the background of his knowledge Nehemiah presented to
the people (especially the groups mentioned in verse 16) a plan
for rebuilding the walls. Nehemiah's own determination, with his
manifest confidence that God's hand was in the undertaking, and
with the encouraging support of the king, gave stimulus to the
people. Their immediate response indicates that the awareness of
need had been present all along, but that capable leadership had
been lacking. When that was supplied "they strengthened their
hands for the good work."

As a forecast of further trouble Sanballat and Tobiah are
again mentioned, this time in company with "Geshem the Arab."
The trio of opponents, either ignorant of the royal support for
Nehemiah's work or pretending ignorance, view this new effort
as rebellion. Nehemiah's reply implies that the three claimed
some rights in Jerusalem, an indication that the Samaritan element was dominant in the opposition.

The Work on the Wall (3:1-32)

Chapter 3 records the work parties and the portions of wall or
gate assigned to each. It moves in regular fashion around the

wall, the "Sheep Gate" serving as point of origin. For the various geographical locations a Bible dictionary should be consulted. The expression "who were under the jurisdiction" is an attempt to make sense of a difficult phrase; another possibility would be that the phrase refers to the locality where the labor was carried on (as vs. 8 and others). The marginal reading of verse 9 is probably correct (see also vs. 18). Verse 12 has a surprising reference to "daughters" participating in the work, although it is not entirely unexpected that women would have taken a share. Another difficult verse is 19, the translation representing at best a guess, as is true of verse 25. The mass of detail and the confusion of names should not blind the Bible student to the fact that here were real people going about a difficult work under adverse conditions and doing so because of their conviction that God had so willed and that his blessing was upon their labor.

Opposition (4:1-23)

The antagonism which had been anticipated in the preceding references to the enemies of the Jews comes to more violent expression. As the work on the wall goes on in earnest it attracts the attention of Sanballat, whose questions (vs. 2) indicate a serious concern. The text of verse 2 is difficult, and the second question is especially uncertain. Tobiah, also mentioned before (2:10, 19), resorts to ridicule.

Nehemiah's reaction is a characteristic blend of prayer and work. The ejaculatory prayer in verses 4-5 is similar to others in this book (for example, 5:19; 6:14). The tone and content are more like some of the Imprecatory Psalms, and, like these, is to be explained by the fact that the authors identified their own work with the purpose of God, hence their enemies as God's. It cannot be denied, however, that Nehemiah's prayer falls short of the New Testament ideal.

Verses 7-12 represent the climax of this stage of the opposition: on the one hand a coalition of neighboring tribes ("Ashdodites" would be dwellers in ancient Philistia), on the other hand the apprehension of the people in Jerusalem, all beautifully and dramatically expressed in a series of quotations—a lament by the community ("Judah"), an exultation by the enemy, and a frightening report by the Jews who lived in districts outside Jerusalem and hence nearer enemy territory.

The measures taken by Nehemiah are well known as an example of practicality wedded to genuine religious faith. Alternation of soldiers with the builders, provision of weapons for the builders themselves, a scheme for rallying all help to a threatened spot, and arrangements for keeping the people from the vicinity in the city overnight, were the practical methods which were strengthened by the steady example of Nehemiah himself (vs. 23) and the faith he expressed and inspired (vss. 14, 20).

Administrative Difficulties (5:1-19)

The account of the difficulties encountered in building the wall is now broken by the report of difficulties of a different kind: those raised by economic and administrative problems. Since chapter 5 deals with an apparently extended period of time, it should be taken as referring to a general situation rather than a single incident occurring exactly during the building of the walls.

A group of the poor expressed to Nehemiah the extreme poverty in which they were forced to live and the fact that under pressure they were compelled first to mortgage their property and then to sell or pledge their offspring to pay debts. Verse 5 emphasizes the equality of members of the community and their unequal positions.

Once again Nehemiah acted as an able administrator. Distressed at this violation of the principles of community responsibility for the poor, he called together the officials. Identifying himself with the ones he charged (vs. 10 indicates that Nehemiah himself had followed the custom of charging interest and taking pledges), he proposed that the custom be dropped and further that there be a wholesale restitution. The principles he followed are clearly set forth in the Deuteronomic law, particularly with reference to the seventh-year restoration (Deut. 15:12-18). "The hundredth" part (vs. 11) which is to be remitted sounds rather low (interest rates ran as high as twenty per cent). Many interpreters, by a slight change of the text, understand instead of this expression "the usury of."

When "the nobles and the officials" agreed to the proposal, Nehemiah sealed the bargain by requiring an oath. The priests administered the oath (vs. 12; see also Ezra 10:5). Finally a dramatic act symbolized the consequence of breaking the oath and provided the people, who had been witnesses, opportunity to add their confirmatory "Amen" (vs. 13; for a parallel to the symbolic action see Job 38:13).

Once again, behind the factual account of an emergency facing the little nation trying to establish itself, we ought to be able to see a profound religious faith at work. Although in the past it is doubtful whether the principles of the restitution of property and release of slaves in the seventh or fiftieth years was ever anything more than an ideal, in this little community it was put into practice, and that by the will of the people themselves. From every vantage point the community impresses the viewer as one anxious to find and do the will of God.

In connection with his testimony to the way he dealt with cases of injustice among the people, Nehemiah adds here the report of his stewardship of the office he held. Two examples are cited (vss. 14, 17-18), which were characteristic of the entire period of his governorship. The first had to do with the fact that he, unlike the earlier officials of the Persian bureaucracy, had not drained the public wealth for the expenses of his office. (The phrase "besides forty shekels of silver" in verse 15 is probably incorrect; something like "at the rate of forty shekels of silver" is called for.) The second example is drawn from his own household and the specific problem of providing food for an immense retinue (the number has been estimated at 400 or 500). For this extraordinary hospitality he had also assumed the financial responsibility.

The Completion of the Wall (6:1—7:4)

Continued Opposition (6:1-9)

Following a time during which the wall itself was finished save for the setting of the gates, the account is resumed with reference again to the difficulties Nehemiah faced from his opponents. The first stratagem they tried was to lure Nehemiah out of the city into possible ambush. This Nehemiah avoided by instant insistence that his work took precedence over all else. Finally the enemies resorted to a psychological attack, interpreting the work on the wall as sign of rebellion against Persia and threatening Nehemiah with exposure to the king as a claimant to the throne of Judah, both serious charges. The "open letter" in which the threats were made may have been intentionally designed to give the greatest possible publicity to the charge, or it may be a term for correspondence written on a piece of pottery. It has been suggested also that the expression "according to this report" (vs. 6) may be a sign of a condensation or summary (like "and so forth"). Sanballat's mention of "prophets" to support the imaginary claim of Nehemiah to be king shows his knowledge of Hebrew history, for in the past prophets had often played just such roles.

Nehemiah indignantly denied the charges and kept about the work. The sentence with which verse 9 ends may be more properly interpreted "And I strengthened my hands," for the appeal to God is lacking in the original.

False Prophets (6:10-14)

What the enemies had wrongly charged against Nehemiah, that he had arranged for prophet support, they themselves were guilty of in reverse. As the story in these verses indicates, one of the stratagems they tried was to hire a friend of Nehemiah to urge him to take sanctuary in the Temple (apparently doing so in a kind of prophetic oracle). The strange expression, "who was shut up" (vs. 10), may refer to a symbolic action by which the false prophet dramatized his appeal to Nehemiah.

Nehemiah's piety and courage are evident, for he refuses the proposal on the grounds that (1) it would be improper for him to enter the Temple and (2) that flight was inappropriate. Verse 12 indicates that *after* his refusal Nehemiah saw through the proposal and understood the evil of Shemaiah. Verse 14 reminds the reader that this incident was typical of many occasioned by false prophets (and at least one false prophetess).

The Completion of the Wall (6:15-19)

In the light of the number of people engaged in the work and the method employed, it is not surprising that only 52 days were required for the whole task. Nehemiah's somewhat laconic report of the completion of his great work does emphasize the effect on the surrounding nations, and the essentially religious character of the undertaking is underlined by the fact that as a result of the completion the nations recognized the hand of God in the work. Thus faithful performance by the Covenant people led to a kind of witness among the peoples to the greatness and grace of God.

There is appended a note concerning Tobiah (vss. 17-19), who by virtue of his marriage was connected with many of "the nobles of Judah." The latter apparently acted as would-be mediators between Nehemiah and Tobiah, on the one hand praising Tobiah to Nehemiah, but on the other giving Tobiah information which he could conceivably use against Nehemiah.

Provisions for the City (7:1-4)

In keeping with his ability as leader, Nehemiah followed the work on the wall with the establishment of an orderly system of defense. This involved the appointment of Hanani his brother (1:2) and Hananiah as rulers of the city. (It has been proposed that for "Hanani and Hananiah" we should understand rather "Hanani, who is Hananiah.") It also involved arranging for the proper care of the gates and a regular watch. The expression "while they are still standing guard" is a guess, for, as the margin indicates, the Hebrew here is uncertain. The method of securing guards is explained by the scarcity of houses in the open spaces of the once destroyed city.

Genealogical List (7:5-73a)

The remark in verse 4 concerning the scarcity of homes leads naturally to the matter of population. Nehemiah's intention to conduct a census led to the discovery of a list of the original company returning to Jerusalem. This list was appended to Nehemiah's memoirs in place of the intended census. It follows in the main Ezra 2:1-70.

RELIGIOUS REFORMATION
Nehemiah 7:73b—10:39

There are numerous ways by which the chronological problems raised by the following section are met. Chief among them is the proposal that all of chapter 8 deals with a continuation of Ezra's reform and belongs there (in I Esdras it appears after the events of Ezra 9). Alternately it has been regarded as a historic account of an additional reform during the time that Nehemiah and Ezra were together in Jerusalem (see 8:9 where they are mentioned together).

Whatever be taken as the solution, it is plain that the memoir of Nehemiah has broken off here, that Ezra rather than Nehemiah is the main character, and that the editor responsible for the compilation of the Book of Nehemiah regarded it as an appropriate fact that the great act of completion of the walls should have been followed by a series of solemn and important religious observances.

The Reading of the Law (7:73b—8:12)

The account of the solemn assembly and Ezra's reading of the Law needs little comment. Although it is marked by a somewhat repetitious style, wholly unlike the Nehemiah memoirs, it is not lacking in lively details. There are certain correspondences to the description of the similar situation during the time of Josiah (II Chron. 34:29-33). "The book of the law of Moses" may be either the Pentateuch or, more probably, selected portions of it. The reading took place on the New Year or the Feast of the Trumpets (Lev. 23:23-25). The length of time required is to be explained by the fact that, as verses 7-8 indicate, there were pauses for explanation.

Nehemiah, designated as "the governor" (see Ezra 2:63), joined with Ezra and the Levites in encouraging the people. The weeping of the multitude may be understood as mourning over the evil which the Law had revealed, or it may have been an emotional reaction to the occasion.

Although the chronology of the event traced here cannot be determined with precision, there can be no doubt that it represented a significant moment in the life of the nation and laid the foundation of the adherence to the Law which so strongly marked later Judaism.

The Observance of the Feast of Tabernacles (8:13-18)

Closer study of the Law by the leaders revealed the failure of the community to observe the prescribed Feast of Booths, or Tabernacles (see, for example, Lev. 23:33-36; Deut. 16:13-15). There followed, consequently, a great reinstitution of the feast, including, as required, the reading of the Law. The remark that such an observance had not been held since "the days of Jeshua [Joshua] the son of Nun" probably refers to the manner rather

than to the actual observance itself. It is likely that at this time
what had been well established in Israel's history became an
urban festival and assumed a new significance in association with
the Law.

The Firm Covenant (9:1—10:39)

The religious ceremonies which celebrated the completion of
the wall are brought to an appropriate climax with the ratification
of a covenant. The reading of the Law, the Feast of Booths, and
now this covenant taken together underline the similarity of the
restoration community to the Hebrews who had departed Egypt
in the first Exodus, heard the Law at Sinai, dwelt in tents in the
wilderness, and entered into solemn covenant with the Lord.

This covenant ceremony was set within a time of fasting and
confession. The Levites are again introduced as officials of the
ceremony. It will be noted that two groups are mentioned in verses
4 and 5, with five names identical and three different. Either
we must suppose that the editor used two sources here and took
over the lists from both or that two different stages in the ceremonies involved different groups with some duplication.

The Revised Standard Version, following the Greek translation, supplies the name of Ezra as the speaker of the long recital
of penitence and prayer beginning in verse 6. Certainly Ezra
might be expected here, because of his prominence up to this
time. And yet it is more likely that the editor appended this material as an appropriate expression of the people's mood of repentance and dedication, and as such meant it to be understood
as spoken by the Levites for the people.

The historical confession moves in orderly and effective fashion
from God's creative act, to the choice of Abraham, the Exodus,
the Covenant at Sinai, the experiences in the wilderness, the Conquest, and the failure of the people to abide by the Covenant. It
affords an excellent example of the way the historical facts of the
Old Testament were read through the eyes of faith as the record
of God's changeless Covenant mercy and the faithlessness of the
Chosen People. Of particular interest and significance for the
situation in the time of Nehemiah is the emphasis on the acts of
God in choosing his people and drawing them into a Covenant
life. The prayer is made up in the main of quotations from Deuteronomy, but they have been assembled in such fashion as to

serve as a miniature theology of the Old Testament in which the
one Actor is God. "Thou art . . . the God who didst choose . . .
and give . . . and didst make . . . the covenant . . . and didst perform signs and wonders . . . didst divide the sea . . . didst come
down . . . and speak." He is the "God ready to forgive, gracious
and merciful."

The prayer ends with a despairing reference to the "great distress" in which the people now live. Verse 38, which reads in the
Revised Standard Version as a sequence to the prayer, signifies
the intention to enter more faithfully into covenant relationship
(although the usual word for "covenant" is lacking here). On
the other hand it is possible that, as in the Hebrew, the verse introduces the material in chapter 10, which originally may not
have been connected with the religious ceremony of chapter 9.

Lists of "those who set their seal" follow in 10:1-27. As he
arranged the material the historian meant it to be understood
that the lists were connected with the solemn covenant ceremony.
Some interpreters believe, however, that it rather refers to some
pledge of reform at another time (note that Nehemiah's name
leads the list but Ezra is not mentioned). The list follows the
order of priests, Levites, and "chiefs of the people."

Finally in verses 28-39 there are specified certain obligations
which were assumed both by the leaders, who either gave their
own seals or witnessed the sealing of the covenantal document,
and by the "rest of the people," including other priests and Levites.
The expression "all who have separated themselves" refers to the
Jews who had not been exiled but who had joined with the returned exiles in rebuilding and in religious reform (see Ezra
6:21).

These all engage in "a curse and an oath" (a covenantal form,
as in Deut. 29:12) with particular respect to avoiding mixed
marriages, to observance of the Sabbath, including the sabbatical
year, and to support of the Temple and its personnel, including
provision of "the tithes." Thus again there are laid the foundations for the Judaism we meet in the New Testament, a Judaism
of particularistic concern, of strict Sabbath keeping, and of central loyalty to the Temple. Included in the required support was
to be "the third part of a shekel," although the original require-
ment called for a half shekel. Along with this went other "contributions" (probably voluntary gifts) and the tithe to be collected
by the Levites, a portion of which went to the priests. It should be

noted that the tithe here refers to vegetable and grain gifts, in harmony with Numbers 18:25-32; nothing is said of herds or flocks as required in Leviticus 27:32-33.

ASPECTS OF THE NEW COMMUNITY

Nehemiah 11:1—13:3

Lists (11:1—12:26)

Here begins a set of miscellaneous materials, without close connection with what immediately precedes. As a matter of fact, the first of the materials, having to do with the settlement of the people in the land, with a proper proportion in Jerusalem, fits better to either 7:4 or 7:73a. Certainly this list is somehow to be associated with the intention of Nehemiah to take a census of Jerusalem, for it is introduced by the purpose to provide one tenth of the population for "the holy city." The names that are given apparently include both those taken by lot and those who "willingly offered to live in Jerusalem."

Then there are appended other lists so that the collection now gives, first, the "chiefs of the province who lived in Jerusalem" (11:3-24); second, the names of the "villages" and the areas in which the Jews lived (11:25-36); and third, "the priests and the Levites who came up with Zerubbabel" together with a body of genealogical information concerning the priests and the Levites (12:1-26).

The first list has resemblances to I Chronicles 9:2-17 although the two have somewhat different settings, which may account for the fact that there are differences of details. The "king" referred to in verses 23 and 24 is probably Artaxerxes, and verse 24 probably implies the presence of Pethahiah at the royal court as a kind of Judean ambassador. The list of priests and Levites in 12:1-11 is mainly parallel to 10:2-8 and less so to 12:12-21, the divergencies indicating that the sources used by the editor were not always precise, that he apparently incorporated his sources without much attempt at harmonization, and that Hebrew nomenclature, like chronology, was a matter which allowed considerable variation and latitude. If "Darius the Persian" is identified as Darius III, the concluding name of "Jaddua" is the high priest who was in office during the reign of Alexander the Great

(333 B.C.). If, on the other hand, it is Darius II, we are pushed back to an earlier time. This would be the beginning of Jaddua's office, or the reference may be to an otherwise unknown Jaddua.

The Dedication of the Wall (12:27-43)

The presence of both the third and the first person pronouns indicates that once again the historian had recourse to the original memoirs of Nehemiah, combining with them another account of the dedication of the newly restored walls of Jerusalem. It is likely that the event here recorded took place soon after the actual completion of the work. The description is of a careful and solemn dedication service and includes an assembly of the people from the surrounding districts, sacrifices of purification, a procession of two companies moving in opposite directions around the city using the broad top of the wall as a walkway, and stated occasions of praise and thanksgiving. In the account Nehemiah is placed in one company and Ezra either at the head of the other company or leading one of its groups. The ceremony is concluded in the Temple with sacrifices and "great joy." The last line of verse 43 is undoubtedly a reference to the loud sound of the ceremony but also reminds one of the prophetic promises concerning the restoration of Jerusalem and its benefits for all nations.

The Worship in the Temple (12:44—13:3)

This short section includes two matters. The first is the description of the service of the Levites and especially of the various measures for the popular support of Temple worship. "On that day" is not meant to identify this material with the immediately preceding day of dedication; rather it is a general expression for an indeterminate time. The rather strange term "according to the fields of the towns" may refer to the manner or the order of collecting the means of support. The mention of Nehemiah indicates that here the editor was not using the memoir of Nehemiah as his source. His purpose seems to have been to draw a picture of ideal worship in an ideal community.

This same ideal character carries over into the second part (13:1-3), where the purity of the religious community is stressed ("the assembly of God" probably refers to the actual religious services). The story of Balaam is found in Numbers 22-24, although the law which was "read from the book of Moses" must have been Deuteronomy 23:3.

NEHEMIAH'S SECOND VISIT TO JERUSALEM
Nehemiah 13:4-31

The remainder of the Book of Nehemiah is concerned with a series of religious reforms instituted by Nehemiah on a second visit to Jerusalem after a stay of some time in Persia. Once again the source was Nehemiah's memoir, as the use of the first person pronoun indicates.

In verse 4 the expression "now before this" indicates that the personal history of Nehemiah is interrupted somewhat suddenly and that "this" is not the incident of 13:1-3 but some incident of the original story, left out by the editor.

There are four main parts of the reforms Nehemiah secured: a purification of the Temple (vss. 4-9), a restitution of support to the Levites (vss. 10-14), a restoration of the Sabbath (vss. 15-22), and a new prohibition against mixed marriages (vss. 23-29).

The first was occasioned by the act of Eliashib (who may have been the same "high priest" mentioned in 13:28 or another, lesser priest) in giving Nehemiah's ancient enemy Tobiah "a large chamber," either for his personal use or as a repository for his goods. Tobiah (see 2:19; 4:3, 7-8; 6:1) was related by marriage to Eliashib but was also an Ammonite (2:10), and hence was excluded from the Temple (13:1). The account of Nehemiah's expulsion of Tobiah on his return to Jerusalem is broken by verse 6, which explains by Nehemiah's absence the fact that such a situation could have developed. The date, "the thirty-second year of Ar-ta-xerxes," would be the twelfth year since Nehemiah's first visit; this date is usually taken as the time of the second visit, allowing twelve years for the first visit and a stay in Persia.

On his second visit Nehemiah found another situation calling for amendment. Although the people had agreed in the solemn covenant to support the Temple personnel (10:37-39), the pledge either had never been fulfilled or had been allowed to lapse. The measures Nehemiah took to deal with the situation and his typical prayer appear in verses 10-14.

In similar fashion verses 15-22 detail the protests Nehemiah made against the breaches of Sabbath observance he found and the practical means he initiated to secure more faithful keeping of the Sabbath. The difficulty of the problem arose from the fact that commerce and trade necessarily involved both Jews and foreigners. The closing of the gates meant not merely that access to the "holy city" was forbidden but also, since it was at the gates that most civic concerns and regular business were transacted, that all labor would cease on the Sabbath.

As would be expected in this time, the two primary concerns of Temple worship and Sabbath observance are joined to a renewed effort in the direction of securing racial and religious purity. Apparently Ezra's reform had not been as entirely successful as the account of it suggests (Ezra 9-10), for here there are reported children of mixed marriages, speaking in foreign tongues. The intensity of Nehemiah's reaction (see also Ezra 9:3) may be partly explained by the enormity of the offense in the light of the previous commitments of the people. The particular instance of "one of the sons of Jehoiada" is mentioned, of course, because of his connection with Sanballat, Nehemiah's old enemy (see, for example, 2:10).

The double appeal with which the book closes—that God "remember" the ones who "have defiled the priesthood" and "remember" Nehemiah "for good"—appropriately brings together the dramatis personae of the whole endeavor: the forces of evil and indifference which might have destroyed the newborn nation and the man of faith and labor who nursed it into a measure of political and religious health. The double appeal also reminds us, however, that even Nehemiah did not stand at the level of the New Testament, as respects the "enemies" and the "friends" of God.

THE BOOK OF
ESTHER

INTRODUCTION

Story

The story of Esther actually exists in two forms, the one preserved in the Hebrew Bible and translated in the Revised Standard Version, and the one in the Greek translation which is the basis for the so-called Additions to the Book of Esther in the Apocrypha.

The Hebrew version is the shorter. It tells the story of the rise of a Hebrew maiden to the position of queen of Persia. By Esther's influence a plot against the Jews is turned against their enemies. The victory of the Jews is celebrated in a day, or two days, of general rejoicing. The story is told as the interplay of political, sociological, and personal factors, with no overt reference to God and no direct suggestion that the religious factors of faith, prayer, and the like played any significant part in the movement of events.

The Greek version is not only longer, it is clearly religiously oriented. The whole story is given a supernatural setting in a dream which forecasts the struggle and victory, and throughout there are interposed references to God and to his working and to prayer and obedience to God on the part of the human participants.

Setting

The original setting and origin of the Book of Esther are difficult to determine. The main clues are to be found in (1) the dating of the book in the time of Xerxes (485-465 B.C.), along with several obviously informed references to the practices of the Persian court and the use of Persian names; and (2) the concern of the book for the proper observance of the Jewish Feast of Purim.

The Persian setting, for all its atmosphere of contemporaneity, involves a great difficulty. Although the name "Mordecai" has been substantiated from extrabiblical records, history does not record the name of Xerxes' queen as Esther, nor does it give reason to suspect any such tremendous struggle between the Jewish people and their Persian neighbors as the book indicates. It seems best, then, to assume that Esther was written well after the time of Xerxes, but still within the Persian period.

Even the casual reader will be impressed by the way the book comes to its climax by insisting on the importance of the Feast of Purim and with prescriptions for its proper observance. This feast has no other substantiation in the Old Testament, being unknown in the Books of the Law, and there being no evidence for its observance before the time of the Exile. Many interpreters believe, therefore, that the feast did not have its origin in Palestine, but in the lands of the dispersion. It is quite possible that it was originally a pagan festival of some kind, which was taken over into Judaism because of the Jews' cultural contacts with the life of their neighbors. It would not be the first nor the last time that such a practice was followed.

We can go a step further and suggest that the book was written to supply for this feast a kind of orthodox Jewish background. The author may well have found ideally suited to his purpose a tradition concerning his heroine and her courageous fidelity to Judaism in the difficult and compromising situation of the Persian court. As was undoubtedly the case with the Book of Job, an ancient story based on a core of authentic fact thus became in the end the vehicle to serve a new purpose.

The Message

The Book of Esther bears close resemblance to one of the books of the Apocrypha, Judith, the story of a Jewish heroine who by her beauty and resourcefulness was enabled to save the Jewish people from the threat of extermination by a foreign oppressor. Although Judith is so religious that Esther appears quite secular in comparison, the two heroines are basically alike in their roles as genuine saviors of their people. Less direct but nonetheless real resemblance exists between Esther and some of the heroes and heroines of Israel's history as recorded in the canonical books. Esther is a spiritual relative of Joseph and

Moses, and especially of Deborah and the other judges. A person who is familiar with the stories of these earlier heroes of faith needs no reminder that Esther is a symbol of God's continuing action to raise up deliverers for his people.

Similarly, although the specific references to God's working are missing in this book, when it is read in the total context of the Old Testament revelation, as it is meant to be read, there is no doubt that it is God's hand that determines the course of affairs. The carefully sustained mood of suspense, the exact working out of events in accord with notions of justice, and the use of seeming coincidences which turn out not to be coincidences at all— these all heighten the sense of the unseen but real Power who determines the entire course of events.

The book is also the expression of a deep conviction that, by God's will, moral principles work themselves out in the world, and particularly in the relationships among people. Evildoers are not merely punished, their punishment is somehow the reverse working of their own evil plans, and stands a witness to their frustrated designs like Haman's gallows, fifty cubits high.

If the Book of Esther seems to dwell unpleasantly on the negative application of this principle and to delight in the misfortunes of the enemies of God's people, we may understand it as a natural reaction of a people who had known little else but unreasoning hostility from their neighbors. We are not, however, to assume that the book allows us the luxury of desiring the destruction of our own real or fancied enemies. Against its mood there stands for the Christian the clear word of the Lord Jesus Christ.

OUTLINE

The Elevation of Esther (1:1—2:23)

The Plot of Haman (3:1—6:13)

The Triumph of the Jews (6:14—9:19)

The Feast of Purim (9:20—10:3)

COMMENTARY

The Elevation of Esther (1:1—2:23)

From the outset the story of Esther evidences a blend of historical fact and fictional elements. On the one hand there is the reference to Ahasuerus, the Hebrew name for the Persian monarch known in history by the Greek form, Xerxes. The extent of his rule, his reign in Susa, which although not the chief capital was a royal residence and a likely place for a royal banquet, the practice of holding such banquets—all these indicate familiarity with the actual situation of the Persian court. On the other hand, the magnitude of the banquet points to the idealized character of the narrative. The inclusion of "the army" as guests (vs. 3, see margin) and the duration for six months recall similar situations in the Apocrypha and also the kind of exaggerated idealization found in the Prologue to the Book of Job.

The name of the queen whose presence was demanded by Ahasuerus, Vashti, does not appear in extrabiblical sources; in fact, Xerxes' queen is known to have been Amestris. The tradition which the author of the story in its present form was using must have been at fault here, or it is possible that the name is correct and the incident was incorrectly associated with the reign of Xerxes.

It is characteristic of the author that he does not engage in extensive character development. Vashti's reason for refusing the royal demand is not stated. The action is swift and conclusive, and the very lack of psychological details amid the manifold elements of physical description has its own literary effectiveness and power.

The deposition of Vashti is recommended by "the seven princes of Persia and Media," a reference to the seven councilors whose attendance on the king is confirmed by historical record. The motivation for the decree strikes the modern reader as somewhat strained, and the conclusion of the matter with the king's order that husbands rule their homes is surely the mark of the storyteller rather than historical fact.

The second chapter initiates the search for a substitute for the deposed Vashti. Although it was apparently the practice of the Persian rulers to choose wives only from the leading families of

Persia, this story speaks of a widespread search for a new royal consort.

Esther is introduced through her cousin, Mordecai. The latter is identified as one of the captives in the deportation under Nebuchadnezzar in 597 B.C. This would clearly imply that Mordecai was a person of high rank, but it is difficult to reconcile the date with the fact that Xerxes' reign came more than a hundred years later. Once again it appears that the author was more familiar with the physical aspects of life in Persia than with the chronological succession of events.

Esther's name is given in its Hebrew and Persian forms. The choice of Esther among the maidens, and especially the way she received first approval and then special and favored treatment, is strongly reminiscent of the Hebrew youths in the story of Daniel (Dan. 1). Esther's partaking of the food of the palace and her later marriage to a foreigner form a great contrast to the insistence on ritual purity that so strongly marks the Book of Daniel and, in a different way, the Books of Ezra and Nehemiah and the apocryphal Book of Judith. It is difficult to say whether the author was actually indifferent to the dietary laws and similar restrictions, or whether the requirements of his story led him to ignore them.

The story of the king's choice of Esther as queen, her coronation, and the customary gifts to celebrate the occasion is told with frankness and heightening interest. Mordecai's part in the venture is not entirely clear, for it is difficult to tell when he had charged Esther not to make her nationality known (2:10) or how he managed to keep up with her situation (2:11). But that he was regarded by the author as a chief character is indicated by the obedience of Esther to his charges, even after she is made queen of Persia (2:20).

Verse 10, which seems to introduce the next event in the story, is a confusing translation of a difficult Hebrew text. The Greek version leaves out this verse. The main interest in the section falls on a plot against the life of Ahasuerus, about which Mordecai was able to supply information. The notice here is anticipation of the turning point of the story in chapter 6. The author makes good use of suspense, as he remarks on the fact that Mordecai's deed was recorded but leaves the reader to puzzle out why no further notice was taken of it.

The Plot of Haman (3:1—6:13)

The stage having been set with the advancement of Esther to a position of privilege and importance, the story now moves to the central issue: the struggle between the would-be persecutors, typified in Haman, and the Jewish people, typified in Mordecai. It is probable that Haman's typical and symbolic character is indicated by his identification as "the Agagite." The traditional understanding of this term, and the most likely, is that it refers to the Agag who was a king of the Amalekites, whom Saul was commanded to destroy (I Sam. 15). The identification is fitting in view of the fact that Mordecai is a descendant of "Kish," the father of Saul (Esther 2:5). It should be noted also that the Amalekites were traditional enemies of the Israelites (see, for example, Num. 24:20). The author of Esther thus exemplified in Haman the type of opposition which the Jews had had to face in the ages past and which they were again facing from some quarter at the time the Book of Esther was written.

This Haman, promoted to the position of premier, or vizier, a position in which he was to be accorded honor and respect from all, is informed that Mordecai, a Jew, refused to join in the universal signs of submission. The text suggests that Haman shared in the ancient, blind antagonism of the Amalekites, for his enmity was directed not only against the one man but against the entire Jewish people, whose destruction he plans.

The date for the execution of Haman's plot is set by lot, and from the Persian word for "lot" the author of Esther derives the name of the Jewish festival of Purim. The phrase "month after month" probably means that those in charge of such procedure went through the months, one by one, until the lot fell on a particular one, and then the same procedure was followed for the days. Thus the twelfth month, Adar, was selected and "the thirteenth day" (3:13) for a general slaughter of the Jews, "a certain people" whose "laws are different." Haman's offer of ten thousand talents is an outright bribe, but the amount is exaggerated, so much so that it is as though the author meant it to be understood as an exaggeration. The king's remark in 3:11 does not mean that the money was returned to Haman; it is an indirect way of accepting the bribe. In 3:15 the author's literary ability is evident as he contrasts the heartlessness of Haman and the indifference of the king with the concern of the people of Susa, where Jews and non-Jews alike are thrown into consternation by the decree.

Although direct references to God are lacking in the Book of Esther, and although there is throughout the book a seeming disregard for some of the ritual requirements of Judaism, it is yet apparent that a deep religious dimension is presupposed in the background. Thus, in chapter 4 Mordecai's mourning and Esther's request for a fast are to be understood as expressions of their religious faithfulness. Esther's hesitance to assume the role Mordecai urged upon her is natural and also intensifies the drama, for the author thus makes it clear that the queen went into real danger in spite of her fears, rather than without fear (see also 4:16). The anticipation of help "from another quarter" (4:14, literally "place") is often taken as an oblique reference to God. If this be true it is the single such reference in the book, although here as elsewhere the activity of God is presupposed. At any rate, the focus of the story is upon the heroine, the human agency through whom, by a combination of almost incredible circumstances, the Jews are to be saved. She is the one who had "come to the kingdom for such a time as this."

In the longer Greek version with its more obvious religious concern, prayers by Mordecai and Esther are inserted at this point. Although by this device the orthodoxy of the book and of its chief characters is indicated, it must be admitted that thereby the story loses in dramatic power.

The dramatic element is now developed by a series of incidents. Esther, who had succeeded in gaining an audience with the king, inexplicably postpones making her request, setting first one banquet and then another. Haman, meanwhile, is described—in terms which magnify his prosperity and power—as moving directly to the public execution of Mordecai. (The specification of a gallows fifty cubits high, that is, about seventy-five feet, is another example of deliberate exaggeration by the author.) The suspense finally is brought to a climax as the king belatedly and apparently accidentally comes to recognize Mordecai's part in saving his life and the fact that the deed has gone unrewarded.

The story at this point begins to turn from tragedy to triumph. First Haman is forced to prescribe royal honors for the one he intends to kill, and Mordecai is given the tokens of royal favor. That this is the beginning of the end is indicated by the remark

of Haman's advisers that if Mordecai is one of the Jews then
Haman will fail in his purpose of destroying him (6:13). This
reversal of their preceding advice (5:14) may be taken as the
dramatic turning point of the book.

The Triumph of the Jews (6:14—9:19)

The climax having been passed, the story moves to its resolution with dispatch, the elements of suspense being now discarded.
The last verse of chapter 6 introduces the denouement and does
so appropriately by stressing the "haste" with which events begin
to move. After the long postponement Esther's request is made,
in which she identifies herself with her stricken people. Although
the meaning of 7:4 is not clear, it appears that Esther here plays
on the idea of having been "sold" and the consequent loss or gain
to the king. It may be that, as the last half of the verse indicates
(understanding "would be" for "is"), she is boldly arguing that
the destruction of the Jewish people would be not only a moral
tragedy but actually a financial loss to the empire, far outweigh-
ing the bribe offered by Haman.

The extent of Haman's involvement in inevitable punishment
is emphasized by the next incident (7:7-8) where, as a result of
another of the seeming coincidences which mark the story but
which are obviously the working out of the divine purpose,
Haman is caught in a compromising situation, his intent completely misunderstood, and his execution is ordered. (The phrase
"they covered Haman's face" may be a reference to a practice of
so indicating a condemned man.) The final touch of ironic justice
is, of course, the reminder of the immense gallows upon which
the persecutor meets his deserved fate.

The reversal of the fortunes of the Jews is similarly exemplified in the story by the figure of Mordecai, who now takes
Haman's place as vizier and adviser to the king. When Esther
again presents a petition to the king it is perhaps to be understood that Haman's plot had not been completely thwarted. Consequently a new edict is prepared which provides that the Jews
may "defend their lives" and as well "annihilate any armed force
. . . that might attack them," and that the Jews may "plunder
their goods" (8:11). As the decree is carried out by the usual
Persian couriers there is recounted the exact reversal of the preceding mourning (8:15-17; see 3:15—4:3) and then the execu-

tion of the decree when, in a day of bloodshed, 500 inhabitants of Susa are slain (9:6). It appears that the author assumes that this massacre is in reaction either to lingering hostility of the kind typified by Haman or even to an outright attack by continuing enemies of the Jews. The account itself, however, does not emphasize the action of the Jews as self-defense but as legitimate retribution upon those whose intent it was to destroy the people of God.

The section closes (9:16-19) with a repeated account of the slaughter, extending it another day in the capital and including in it a tally of the total slain (the number is considerably smaller in the Greek version). This section probably was intended to explain the fact that observance of the Feast of Purim varied from the fourteenth of Adar to the fifteenth of Adar. Verse 19 identified the variation as presumably a matter of residence in rural or urban areas.

The Feast of Purim (9:20—10:3)

The connection of the Book of Esther with the Feast of Purim is clear in the closing section of the book. Here the preceding story is emphasized as giving support to the observance of the feast for which there was no authority in the Law of the Old Testament, and its name is associated with the incidents recorded in the book. Since the feast lacked canonical authorization it is substantiated by the joint letter of Mordecai and Esther, both of whom are designated as of particular authority, the one by his connection with the "power and might" of Ahasuerus, the other as queen. Their letter or letters (it has been proposed that "this second letter" in 9:29 refers to the present Book of Esther) direct the continual observance of the feast (9:28) and give directions concerning it (9:22).

The section summarizes the whole account of Esther's intervention for her people and follows the motif of the entire book in reiterating the fact that Haman was an Agagite, thus making solid the relationship to the past and confirming the symbolic character of the man as "the enemy of all the Jews."

THE BOOK OF

JOB

INTRODUCTION

As is the case with most great literature, and with all literature of revelation, it is far better to read the Book of Job than to read about it. The only justification for an "introduction" to this masterpiece is either to explain obscure points (which might more conveniently be dealt with in the actual comment) or to remove misconceptions which bar understanding. These pages attempt the latter purpose under three main heads: What the book is, where it comes from, and what seems to be its purpose.

What Is the Book of Job?

Contents

Before reading any further it would be well for the student to leaf through the Book of Job in order to note its basic structural pattern. A cursory examination shows that the book is a long poetical composition, embraced by a prose introduction (or Prologue) and a prose conclusion (or Epilogue). Closer examination of the poetry also reveals that it follows a fairly even pattern. There are various participants who speak in turn, and there is a regularity about the order of their speeches. The pattern of speeches appears in chapters 3-14 (see 3:1; 4:1; 6:1; 8:1; 9:1; 11:1; 12:1), and much the same pattern is repeated in chapters 15-21. Similar marks of regular structure appear at 27:1; 29:1; 32:15; and especially at 40:1-5; 40:6; and 42:1-6. All of this can be easily seen, and to take note of it gives some preparation for an intelligent reading of the book as a whole.

The Character of the Book of Job

Acquaintance with the form of this book raises the more basic question of its nature. Precisely what is it? Is it drama or epic poetry, to use two of the most common designations? Is it a debate, as the pattern of speeches seems to suggest? Although at first glance such defining terms may seem to be appropriate, all fall short on closer look. The truth is that the Book of Job resists categorizing of this kind. It is not a modern production; it came out of a culture which knew neither drama nor debate in the modern sense of the terms. It has dramatic touches, it has elements of argument, and it has undeniable epic power. But to think of it in any of these accustomed and familiar patterns is to miss the important fact that it is unique. Long ago it was pointed out that one of the greatest difficulties posed by the Book of Job is precisely the fact that it has no parallels. There is nothing with which to compare it. We should not expect to find here the familiar and the recognizable; instead we may look for a strange and somewhat alien treatment of themes that are universal.

Poetic Forms

It is generally known that, whereas Hebrew poetry does not make much use of rhyme, it does build on regular metrical forms in a simple structure of parallel lines. Often strophes or verses are present, as is particularly true of parts of Job.

The metrical patterns of the Book of Job are quite varied, reflecting most of the forms found elsewhere in Scripture. Sometimes the length and character of the lines in the English translation reflect the actual metrical pattern, although these patterns are by no means identical with the familiar arrangement of feet in Western poetry.

Parallelism is more important, and fortunately it is a readily observable feature of Hebrew poetry. Parallelism is immediately apparent, for example, in Job 29:3, 8, 14, and 17, where each verse presents a single thought in slightly altered form in two successive lines. The image and the actual phraseology change, but in each case the second line is basically a repetition of the first.

Sometimes the parallelism of lines is not that of identical statement but of opposites, where a truth is elaborated by a positive and then by a negative statement (see, for example, 5:3; 36:6). At other times the thought is developed in lines of continuing repetition (3:5, 6) or by lines that expand a stated thought (5:4). It is always helpful to the reader of the poem to keep this feature in mind, and even to learn to feel the poetic force of regularly repeated statement.

How Did the Book of Job Originate?

Background

Although there are no close parallels to the Book of Job which can serve as convenient points for comparison or contrast, this is not to say that it has no relationship to other literary developments of antiquity. Resemblances in structure, in type of expression, and even in basic themes can be found between the Book of Job and Egyptian and Babylonian writings. In no case is there any evidence of borrowing or even of direct dependence, but similarities of form and theme do point to similar concerns among other peoples and even to similar methods of literary approach to common problems.

A more fruitful line of study, and one open to all students of this book, is the investigation of the relationship Job bears to other writings within the Old Testament. Although in format it is completely unlike any of the other books, its origin and its particular concerns are to be understood in the light of the issues raised in the so-called "wisdom writings," particularly the Book of Proverbs and, to a lesser extent, the Book of Ecclesiastes. Such writings are the work of a "school" or a class of "wise men" in ancient Israel. Differing from both prophet and priest, the wise man was nevertheless like both in that his concern was a religious one. The wise men undertook, on the one hand, to apply the revelation of God made to Israel in history and in the Law to the minutiae of everyday life, much as the prophets did to the broader and more comprehensive areas of society. On the other hand, the wise men also undertook to explore the *meaning* of life, again much as the prophets explored the meaning of history. In so doing, they followed out the implications of the faith with which the Bible opens and which Israel always regarded as foundational —the faith that life itself is the direct creation of God who pronounced it good, and that it must therefore carry some marks of his nature.

In the Book of Proverbs, especially in the central part (chs. 10-29), certain basic presuppositions emerge. These are nowhere stated absolutely, but they do appear to be working hypotheses so far as the wisdom writers were concerned. Among these presuppositions are the following:

1. The belief that life, that is, the realm of human life and

experience, makes sense. This somewhat incredible belief was seriously challenged in the Book of Ecclesiastes, but it remained a constant of Israelite faith. Any other view, of course, would be unthinkable, given the fact of creation. We must notice especially, however, that for the Hebrew to say that life makes sense means primarily not philosophical or metaphysical sense or even rational sense, but *religious* sense.

2. The belief that, as a corollary to the above, God himself can be known through the events and happenings of life. God is everywhere in control; his hand orders all small events as he directs the course of history. It follows, then, that by a reverent and careful study of such happenings one may draw some conclusions concerning the nature of God.

3. The belief that *this* life, not another future one, is the sphere in which God makes himself known for blessing or for punishment. With few exceptions, the basic wisdom writings show no belief in a future life of any consequence. The issues that develop and the questions that are raised by the evidence that life offers must necessarily be resolved within the narrow span of a man's life, threescore years and ten.

4. The belief that moral principles not only work out in life but indeed can be discerned as they work. Specifically this means that goodness in man is rewarded appropriately with blessings and that evil in man is visited with punishment. This belief, which is basic to any sensible view of God, was of course the foundation of much of the prophets' view of history. But whereas the prophets had a broad canvas upon which to work—namely, the whole scope of national and political life—the wisdom writers confined themselves largely to the narrow limits of man's individual life.

It is easy to see how these principles and others like them, when applied too rigidly, produced more questions than answers. They are *general* truths, agreed to by the great body of Old Testament writers, from Moses through the prophets and the psalmists. They fail, however, as exact formulae when *every* experience of life is made to fit their scheme. The dilemmas which the Book of Job faces so realistically, then, are the dilemmas posed by these principles. Thus they are the dilemmas of faith. To a man unconcerned with faith the Book of Job has no appeal save a superficially aesthetic one. Even to one who is absolutely secure in faith it has nothing to say; it may, in fact, appear to such a one as something of an embarrassment. It speaks, however, to those who know the difficulties of faith, who know that believing often raises more questions than it answers, and who *because* they believe are driven on in the search to know.

Date and Author

What, then, was the time when such problems became most acute and to which, therefore, we may most naturally assign the Book of Job? An easy answer cannot be had. The most natural time would be the Exile, especially in the period when that time of testing and distress for the Jews began to come to its close. But any attempt to find an exact date, or even to declare with confidence that the book originated in the Exile, is as barren of success as the attempt to find the author. It fits many ages of Israel's history, for it is a book that speaks to a crisis and there were few ages when Israel was not faced with crisis.

Of the author we may say that he was a genius, that he was a great theologian of the grace of God, that he was an unexcelled poet. But his identity is lost; he has left no clue in his book, and history provides none.

The Parts of the Book

To use the term "the author" is somewhat misleading. Most interpreters of the Book of Job feel that, at least in its final form, it is the work of more than one hand and mind. And as will be indicated in the comment, there is much evidence that points in this direction, notably in connection with the speeches of Elihu, part of the speeches of the Lord, and the Prologue and Epilogue.

It is quite reasonable to assume that so far as the Prologue and Epilogue are concerned we have to do with a very old story, which the author utilized as a setting for his discussion. In so doing, however, he must have reworked it to make it blend in some respects with his own work.

It is reasonable also to say that near the end of the book the author or a later editor, or even a group of wise men, incorporated into the body of the original work other material, composed independently but contributing to the central themes. The important thing, of course, is that as a *final* work the book has great power, and that as a unit it finds its place in Scripture. Certainly it is to be studied first of all as a unit. It can be said with confidence, moreover, that of all attempts to better the structure of the Book of Job by rearrangement of its parts or by omission of some, none comes anywhere near equalling the power of the whole as it stands today.

The Message of the Book

Literary Values

Although aesthetic appreciation is not the primary purpose of any Bible study and although a proper understanding of the message of the Book of Job has often been hampered by excessive preoccupation with its literary character, still one would be unusually blind and deaf not to value the book as literature. Besides his power as a poet, the author shows his creative ability in countless ways. For example, while character delineation was not the author's main purpose, the fact remains that Job, his friends, and Elihu all are given clear portrayals without a line of description.

The author has his own way of achieving literary effect, a method not at all in harmony with standards accepted in the modern age under the influence of Western models of literature. Throughout the book, for example, there is an evident pattern of climax followed by a kind of quiet falling off. Where we would expect the climax of separate speeches and even of the work as a whole to come at or near the end, in this book most of the climactic material occurs in the middle of a speech or a division. (See, for example, the climactic words in 19:23-27, followed typically by an anticlimactic section.)

In keeping with what seems to be deliberate intent, the book also follows a strange pattern of dealing with ideas as they are advanced in the discussion. An idea is advanced and then apparently ignored for a time, to be taken up again later on and either expanded or refuted at that point. Motifs appear and reappear in this fashion so markedly that one necessarily thinks of some sort of cyclic arrangement of material rather than a straight-line progression from beginning to end.

Major Themes

Just as no one descriptive term fits the Book of Job as a definition, so no one statement can describe its contents and purpose. Certainly it is a great misapprehension to imagine that its single theme is the problem of suffering. There are many themes

which are woven into one another. Among them are the following, along with others that will be discussed in the comment
and still others that will doubtless appear to the observant reader.

1. There is the theme stated in the Prologue and the Epilogue
as these are taken together without the intervening discussion.
This is the idea that there exists such a thing as "disinterested
goodness" and that Job is a good example of it. This was the
point of the ancient story which the author utilized, and it is
surely a point that needs constant reiteration, especially in an age
which is apt to set materialistic criteria of success for every venture of life, even faith. Against such a view this old story raises
its protest, holding up for admiration a single individual who held
on to his integrity and faith, even though instead of success these
qualities seemed to bring him only failure and tragedy.

2. There is the bold denial of an absolute application of the
principle of rewards and retribution. Without denying the fact
that moral principles do operate in the world, the book nevertheless forbids any tendency to catalogue all human experience by
such a rule (see also in Luke 13:1-3 and John 9:1-3 Jesus' denial of the same tendency). The poet does not deny that there is
a connection between righteousness and blessing and between sin
and tragedy, but he does deny that it can be reasoned out on the
basis of life's evidences.

3. There is the strong emphasis on firsthand knowledge of
God. In the place of the reasoned orthodoxies of the friends, in
the place of Job's own efforts at rational explanation of his experience, there stands at the end only this one fact: God himself
meets man. In that meeting he neither answers man's questions
nor gives him the kind of peace he seeks and believes to be his
deepest need, but because God is there neither questions nor that
kind of peace seems to matter very much.

4. There is the breaking open of the possibility of a future life.
This is put forward in the book only on individual terms, and
then somewhat tentatively, but for Job to have posited it at all
was a real advance upon the common expectation of a meaningless existence after this life, for which Sheol stood as the bleak
symbol. In Job there is not yet the full light of the New Testament, but it is not amiss to say that in this book there shines the
first clear ray of the Easter dawn.

5. There is the depth of understanding of human sin. Beyond
all *sins* we deal here with the primeval sin, that of rebellion

against God. All of the human participants in the discussion participate in that sin. Each in his own way makes God in his own image (an insight that William Blake has clearly seen in his "inventions" on the Book of Job). Each is unwilling for God to be God on his own terms, and each in the end must stand before the God who is God, and who does not exist only in man's definitions or man's experiences. He is the God who defines himself, with a definition that immediately contradicts all others.

6. There is the evident fact that with all of Job's wrongness *he* is the hero of faith. His doubt is the reflex of true faith, far more so than is the theologizing of the friends. And it is Job who is vindicated for his insistence that knowledge of God be somehow observable within the arena of this life. Job never leaves the realm of his own existence and never gives up the demand that God be known, not in some essentially supernatural vision or some purely heavenly manifestation, but within the frame of his own life. And he is right. The fact that the Lord speaks at the end in a whirlwind ought not to be construed as a pure "supernaturalism." The point is that God *speaks*, speaks the language that Job knows, converses with him, and makes himself known by pointing to evident facts of life. Job, it must be said, is in many ways the strongest witness in the entire Old Testament to the Incarnation, for in his agony he never gives up the conviction that finally God must be known within the intimate realm of our life. Even Job cannot anticipate what will be the blinding glory of the Son of God who "became flesh," but he knows *where* the glory of the Father must be revealed.

7. There is, above all else in this book, a true note of the grace of God. For all his abundant righteousness and his integrity, Job was still sinner (would he not have understood Paul's "chief of sinners"?). And the point is that to such a man, a kind of Adam in rebellion against his Maker, God comes in mercy and grace. The basic faith of the book is that Job, who above all else wished to be justified, learned that the way to justification is not by self-justification but by God's justifying grace. Justification is not something we achieve (to use the Protestant formula), nor is it something we establish for ourselves (to use Job's formula); it is God's gracious gift. Job and Paul are more alike than any other biblical characters. The thing that separates them is that Paul knew in *whom* God justifies the ungodly.

OUTLINE

COMMENTARY

THE PROLOGUE

Job 1:1—2:13

The story which now stands as a prose introduction and a prose conclusion to the Book of Job can be read in two ways. It can be read for itself, apart from the poetical discussion, and indeed this is the way it undoubtedly once existed. Or it can be read in connection with the discourses, preparing the way for them although not explaining them.

In itself this is the story of a wise, good, pious, and immensely prosperous man who suffered the loss of all the blessings that had once been his; who, in addition, suffered the most grievous blows in body and spirit; and who yet maintained an unshaken trust in God. In a religious culture which necessarily regarded material benefits as rewards of true religion (see Introduction) the story performed a valuable function, for it keeps the order between faith and its rewards straight. Benefits are the *result*, but they are not of the essence of faith. Job's story shows that here is one man who does not make faith depend upon its results, who does not reverse the basic truth into untruth. His goodness, the story indicates, was "disinterested goodness," neither dependent upon rewards nor destroyed when blessing turned into loss. In the end (see the Epilogue) the benefits reappeared, for the story makes it plain that there *is* a connection between goodness and rewards. But the connection is not mechanical, and quality of life and trust do not depend upon its exact working.

The second way the story can be read is as background for the discussion in 3:1—42:6. Undoubtedly the story had long been in existence when the unknown author of the present book saw in it an ideal setting for the theological discussion he wished to present. We may assume that he took this ancient tale, the theme of which must have been familiar to many people, and gave it a new direction. It became then not simply the story of a good man who maintained his goodness and his faith when the usual and expected benefits were taken away. Whereas the original story in a real sense focused on Job, in the light of the poetic discussion which is introduced it now centers on God. For its major significance now is to serve as a prelude to a theological discussion, raising the whole question of the nature of God in whose world tragedies such as Job's do happen, and the even more personal question of the relationship between God and man in the light of the undeniable facts of human existence.

The Prologue alternates between earth and heaven in its scenes, building up to a great climax. It has many stylized and somewhat formal elements, indicating that it had taken shape first of all in the process of ancient storytelling.

The First Scene on Earth (1:1-5)

The locale is "the land of Uz," which is probably to be identified with a portion of the land of Edom (other elements in the book are associated with the same land). The protagonist is "Job," whose name may mean "hated" or perhaps "penitent." The name occurs again in Ezekiel 14:14 and 14:20, where it is connected with "Noah" and "Daniel," and where Job, along with the others, is taken as an example of righteousness.

The tradition of Job's righteousness is elaborated in the first scene of the Prologue, where he is described in honorific terms. First, as to his character, he is "blameless and upright." The former term is used of other Old Testament characters (Gen. 6: 9; 17:1), and although it does not imply absolute perfection it does refer to blamelessness in connection with God's demands. It is essential to note that this blamelessness on the part of Job is never seriously questioned, save by his three friends, who are proved to be wrong. In the next scene God himself puts his seal on the perfection of Job, and throughout the book it is taken for granted. Thus at the outset we are warned against the natural disposition to "explain" all that happened to Job on the basis of his sins.

Matching Job's perfection of life, both in relation to God and in relation to man (vs. 1), there is perfect prosperity. Job's family and his holdings are described in ideal terms (note the numbers 7 and 3, 5 and 5). Finally, to this picture of perfection there is added the note of perpetual joy, symbolized in a round of feasts at the houses of the seven sons. Externally these verses provide a description of a great chieftain or sheik in a nomadic land (although such features as "the house" do not exactly fit the nomadic atmosphere). But the story essentially demonstrates the

truth that fearing God and turning away from evil constitute
precisely the *good life*.

Job's piety is further illustrated by his repeated acts of sacrifice.
Is there a note of superstitious fear here, in that, although he did
not know of any evil wrought by his children, he made burnt
offerings for them? Is he fearful lest something happen to disturb
the even and happy tenor of life? Such a fear would not be unexpected and would not in any sense detract from the genuine
piety that is pictured here.

The First Scene in Heaven (1:6-12)

The antiquity of the story which the author of the Book of Job
uses as his setting is indicated by the bold way in which it pictures a heavenly council that includes one rather disreputable
member. It is also significant that the author apparently uses the
story without change, although he undoubtedly would not himself have accepted some of its implications. At any rate, to balance the preceding picture of piety and calm prosperity there is
now presented a scene of foreboding. The "sons of God" are to
be understood as semidivine beings, perhaps angels (see 38:7;
Gen. 6:2; Ps. 89:6). "Among them," that is, as one of their group,
there was also "Satan" or more properly "the Satan." The term
is probably not to be understood as a proper name but as a descriptive word (see margin). It is clear that although in an ultimate sense this being can be identified with "the devil" of Christian tradition, he is not so conceived here. The Old Testament in
general has no concept of an evil being in opposition to God, although its sense of powerful chaotic forces held in check by God
presages such a figure. Here "the Satan" is represented as the
adversary not of God but of man, and his concern is to reveal the
flaw in human nature (see a similar picture in Zech. 3:1-5).

The Satan poses the challenge: Job is not good "for nothing."
His piety is simply insurance against loss. His goodness will
evaporate if the benefits it brings are removed. God accepts the
challenge with an astounding faith in man, or at least in Job.
Within limits, which are carefully set by God, the Satan is now
permitted to test Job—to "touch all that he has."

The Second Scene on Earth (1:13-22)

The "day" of the heavenly council (vs. 6) is now paralleled by another "day" (vs. 13). This day, which is pathetically described as a day of feasting, brings between dawn and evening total loss and total tragedy. The horror of the happenings is heightened by the fact that they follow one another without cessation. Flocks, herds, servants, and children are taken from Job with a single blow.

The scene ends with Job, unshaken in his trust in God, still worshiping, and not charging God with "wrong." The man of faith is reduced to mourning, his only prospect is emptiness, but he still cries, "Blessed be the name of the LORD." God's faith in his servant Job is justified.

The Second Scene in Heaven (2:1-6)

But Job is to be yet more severely tried. The Satan explains his failure on the basis of the fact that Job's own body has not yet been touched. In a declaration which in countless lives has been proved to be a lie the Satan makes man out to be incurably selfish. "Skin for skin" has come to be a proverbial expression, and such it must have been at the time the story was current. It is not clear now just what the imagery is, although a good guess is that it refers to an ancient system of bartering hides, so that the meaning may be that a man will pile up all his possessions (and even his family) on one side to save his own life from harm.

Again the Satan is allowed to go forth against Job and "touch his bone and his flesh," but again it is within certain limits ("only spare his life").

The Third Scene on Earth (2:7-13)

When we turn from the presence of the Lord to Job, this time we see the blameless and righteous man stricken with a fatal and loathsome disease, the honored chieftain turned into an outcast and forced to live on the heap of dung ashes. The description of his disease here and elsewhere (see 7:5; 30:30) and especially the fact that he is reduced to the life of an outcast point to the possibility that Job is smitten with leprosy. Certainly some serious skin disorder is meant, although the popular notion that he had boils is far from the mark.

The part that Job's wife plays has always been a matter of conjecture. Is she his true sympathizer, who because she cannot bear the sight of his suffering counsels him to take the quick way out? Or is she, as one of the early interpreters said, "the last instrument of the devil," in that she urges Job to give up his now apparently discredited and useless faith? The most that can be said with certainty is that she, who was spared to Job in the otherwise complete tragedy that befell his family, is still no real help. His alienation from all mankind is becoming complete, symbolized especially in this misunderstanding on the part of the one closest to him.

In verses 11-13 the stage is finally set for the discussion. Three friends who, like Job, were honored wise men come to comfort him. They are represented as coming from lands of the East (Teman is in Edom, and both "Shuhite" and "Naamathite" point to nomadic tribes on the borders of Palestine). Although the tragedy Job has suffered has so completely changed him that at first the men cannot recognize their friend, they join in true and sympathetic mourning.

Once again as the scene closes we are faced with the ultimate in human suffering and despair, and yet also with the ultimate in trust and faithfulness. Job still did not sin with his lips. Against this remarkable background there now opens an even more remarkable scene, where in place of mourning there comes wild rebellion, and in place of the silence of Job there sounds the most extreme shout of protest.

THE FIRST ROUND OF DISCUSSION

Job 3:1—14:22

Job Speaks (3:1-26)

Out of the depths there comes a cry of despair. It is all the more shocking when it is heard against the background of the glad faith with which the Scriptures open. In the creation story (Gen. 1:1—2:4a) it is a fundamental point that when God created life he saw that "it was good." Men were to live in the midst of this good life, accepting its goodness as God's blessing and finding in its order and beauty signs of his presence and favor.

To reject life, then, amounts to a rejection of God; to curse life is to blaspheme; even to deny that life is good is virtual denial of God. All this and worse Job now does, as he breaks out, first in a curse on the day of his birth or conception (vss. 1-10), then in an agonizing wish that he had perished at birth (vss. 11-19), and in a plea that he be given death now (vss. 20-26). The entire chapter has close resemblances to the cry of another troubled soul, Jeremiah, when he found his life almost unbearable (Jer. 20:14-18).

A Curse on the Day I Was Born (3:1-10)

"It would have been better if I had not been born!" So Job begins his complaint, declaring that had he been given a choice, he would have chosen nonbeing rather than the kind of existence he must now endure.

The language is full of images which are not, of course, to be taken literally. The basic image throughout this section is that of darkness which overcomes and obscures the day. So Job imagines the day on which he was born and the night in which he was conceived as both so overwhelmed in thick darkness and blackness that they had never come to be numbered with the other days of the year (vss. 5-6).

Job fancifully calls upon sorcerers who supposedly could blot out the day by their curses. The reference to "Leviathan" in verse 8 may be to the serpent which, in many ancient cultures, was thought to cause eclipses by swallowing the sun, although there is no other trace of such belief among the Hebrews. More probably it is the symbol of the primeval chaos which was overcome by God as he brought about the order of creation. To "rouse" this ancient sea monster would be to destroy the even order of days in the calendar. The poetic image, "the eyelids of the morning," stands for the slanting rays of the rising sun. The reason for Job's passionate curse is finally stated in verse 10.

If Only I Had Died at Birth! (3:11-19)

In the second part of Job's initial protest verses 11, 12, and 16 set forth his wish that he had perished at birth. Since it is manifestly impossible to remove the day of his birth from the calendar, the next best thing would be for Job to have been as an infant that had never seen the light.

The remainder of the section is a calm, somewhat wistful statement of the imaginary consequences of such early, untimely
death. Here is one of the longest and most detailed pictures of
"Sheol" to be found in the entire Old Testament (see also Pss.
6:5; 88:4-12; 115:17; Eccles. 9:10; Ezek. 32:17-32). The most
prominent aspect of this region of the dead is emphasized in verse
13, where four successive verbs stress its "quiet" and "rest." We
would be greatly mistaken, however, if we were to identify this
with the peace of true eternal life. Although the picture of Sheol
here bears a startling resemblance to some common expectations
of heavenly bliss, Sheol itself was never regarded as a state of
blessedness. To the Hebrew, strong in his faith that God had
created life and that God made his presence known in life, to be
deprived of life was no blessing. And Sheol, as this passage makes
abundantly clear, was not life. It was, indeed, a kind of existence,
for annihilation seems never to have been considered as a possibility by the Hebrews, but because God was not known there,
and because he did not work his wonders there, it was a kind of
existence to be abhorred. That Job dreams of it with such apparent longing is tantamount to blasphemy. The normal cry of the
Old Testament man of faith was, "Bring me not to Sheol!" Here
a righteous, faithful man *desires* Sheol, and that itself is the
strongest witness to the agony of his present life.

Verse 14 is obscure. The reference may be to the practice of
building new cities on the ruined heaps of former ones. Or the
"ruins" may be the capital cities of ancient conquerors, which
once were "rebuilt" but have again been destroyed. In either case
the main point is that in Sheol all distinctions are done away;
"the small and the great are there."

This passage, it should be noted, gives the reader a clear understanding of one important aspect of Job's problems. Whatever
solutions are to be found, it is obvious that they must be found in
this *present* life, not in the next. That is, they must so be found
unless some new insight or some new revealing can, for Job, re-
place the gray, shadowy outlines of Sheol.

I Wish I Were Dead! (3:20-26)

The idea of "light" binds the three parts of Job's opening so-
liloquy into a unity (see vss. 9, 16). In this last section it reap-
pears in a passionate question: "Why is light given?" The same
question, although absent in the Hebrew, must be understood in

verse 23. Another unifying theme is to be found in the contrast of verse 26 with verses 13 and 17, where the repetition of words emphasizes the difference between Job's troubled state and the rest of Sheol.

In this last section the climax of Job's protest is reached. The question is now practical and immediately relevant: Why is life continued, since it offers no peace but only multiplied troubles? Job longs for death, expressing his desire in sharp images, each one underlining the bitterness of his soul, his doubts about the goodness of life, and his conviction that he has been forsaken by God.

Troubles and accompanying complaints are always before Job; like bread and water, they are his constant diet. Finally, in a last pathetic reference to his own situation, he cries that his anxieties, instead of being shown to be false, always prove to be forerunners of actual adversity. The fears devised by his imagination come to be very real happenings, so that over his whole existence are to be written the words: "Trouble comes."

Chapter 3 of Job is one of the outstanding poetic constructions of the whole book, in fact, of all the Old Testament. It is a classic statement of the "dark night of the soul," one unrelieved cry of anguish. And the depth of disaster from which the cry ascends is not at all the loss of either possessions or prestige; it is the loss of meaning. For Job it involves the loss of the sense of God's presence and blessing. The true dimensions of his problems are yet to be revealed, but they are implicitly here. Here is a man for whose despair only God can provide an adequate remedy, but whose despair itself seems to come from God. God is his problem.

Eliphaz Speaks (4:1—5:27)

You Know the Answer to Your Problems (4:1-11)

Although it becomes more pronounced as the discussion develops, already in the first speech of Eliphaz there is evident a tendency to talk beside the point. The impression throughout is that the friends, as they talk, are not really considering either Job or his contention. This is certainly no argument or debate in the modern sense of the terms. The friends are like men who close their eyes to the real facts, rock back on their heels, and speak of general principles, every one of which is being called into serious question by the indisputable facts before them. Job is like a man crying out, "Look at me! I am the evidence in this dispute." To his cry, however, the friends remain deaf.

Eliphaz begins with some gentleness and consideration. Never a fully sympathetic figure, here at least he is less harsh than later. His opening words may be taken as a kind of half apology for the fact that he must speak at all; that he speaks is due only to the extremes of Job's preceding statements. Eliphaz has been a quiet sympathizer as long as Job has kept patient silence. But now that Job has expressed his violent longing for death, such impiety and implicit blasphemy cannot be ignored.

Moreover, as verses 4-6 show, Eliphaz needs only, in his view, to remind Job of the principles which operate in his case. They are the very principles which Job himself has used many times to strengthen others who were in danger of falling into skeptical despair. Job is forgetting the bedrock principle upon which he has always stood and to which he has pointed others. That principle, of course, is the fact that faith and integrity of life are, in the long run, rewarded by happiness and peace. The "fear of God" mentioned in verse 6 is literally "fear" and may be understood as a synonym for "religion" or "faith." Job's future is not uncertain, and he can face it with confidence and hope.

Eliphaz obviously recognizes that some sort of disaster has actually come upon Job (in verse 5 the thing that has happened is neither named nor described), but he also obviously believes that it is a temporary matter and only a seeming exception to the general rule.

In verses 7-11 considerably more attention is given to the negative side of the principle which Eliphaz holds out for Job's comfort. His question in verse 7 is evidence again of his utter disregard of Job's actual situation. Eliphaz reassures Job that he will not die in untimely fashion; Job wants nothing more than to die now! Death, to Eliphaz, would be confirmation of wickedness; to Job it would be a mercy.

Eliphaz' position is clear: Trouble is the harvest of iniquity. Wicked men are destroyed in the wrath (breath) of God. They are like dangerous lions (there are four separate Hebrew words for "lion" in verses 10 and 11), but they are deprived of their power and they come to ruin.

Only the Wicked Man Is Insecure (4:12—5:7)

After confidently citing the facts of life as he sees them, Eliphaz next makes appeal to a kind of private revelation which he has been permitted to receive. Verses 12 through 21 are unique in the Bible in that they speak of a ghostly communication of a divine message. It must be remembered that the friends, although they often speak true words, are not the vehicle of all truth, and some of their views are definitely wrong. Normally in the Bible the word of God came to his spokesmen in a much more straight-forward fashion, and their descriptions of its coming are usually clear and uncomplicated. Eliphaz' account is suited to the experience it describes; it is involved and mysterious, promising a great deal more than it actually delivers.

The speaker represents special knowledge as coming to him at night, when most men are asleep, although he apparently was fully awake. He was seized with a great dread as a wind passed before him. ("Wind" is a better translation in verse 15 than "spirit.") The apparition which accompanied the wind is not clearly described or seen, being called "it" and "a form." But through the silence a voice spoke, and although quiet and whispering (vs. 12) it was clear.

Its message, it must be admitted, was not startlingly profound. Nor, given the Old Testament revelation, was it necessary that such a message be delivered privately to Eliphaz. It is the basic truth that in comparison with God himself no man can be accounted righteous or morally clean (vs. 17). Relatively speaking, man is not as righteous as God. This truism, for so it is, does not speak at all to the fact of Job's case, where the questions have to do not with man's *absolute* righteousness before God but with man's "integrity" and his faithful performance of the commands of God. Moreover, as Eliphaz develops the thought, or as the ghostly appearance continues, the immediate effect of such a view, if it is allowed to dominate theology and life, is to remove God farther and farther from man, and to set a complete, impassable gulf between an almighty divine Perfection, and frail, finite man.

In verses 18 and 19 the argument proceeds in this very direction, as the point is made that if God is more righteous than angels (his spiritual servants), how much more righteous he is than man. From here on, there follows a series of tragic word pictures of the transience and frailty of men who dwell in "houses of clay, whose foundation is in the dust." Man's life is crushed out like a moth's (rather than "before the moth"); it is so short that it is spent between one morning and the same evening; and, worst of all, the end comes "without any regarding it." Is God included in this "any"? If so, then Eliphaz' strict and orthodox monotheism has led him into deism, with a god so remote from man that he neither cares nor notices. If the "any" refers only to man, it is still profoundly pessimistic. The words of Eliphaz run counter to the whole movement of the Old Testament, where both life and death are determined by the will of God and where both take place in his presence. If the Revised Standard Version translation of verse 21 is correct, the image is shifted from the frail house of clay which is man's dwelling, to the tent of a nomad which is never permanent. More probably the word for "tent-cord" should be translated "excellence." The meaning of the verse then would be that whatever advantage or superiority man has is terminated at death, and when man dies his claim to wisdom dies with him.

In close connection with his private vision Eliphaz goes on to describe in some detail the unhappy and ephemeral life of wicked men. His concentration on evil man, in close connection with his view of God's transcendent righteousness and man's frailty, suggests that verses 19-21 also concern the wicked, rather than man in general.

The opening verse of chapter 5 is abrupt. The "holy ones" are angels; Eliphaz thus is inquiring whether Job intends to rely on such beings as intermediaries in his dispute with God. If so, Eliphaz implies, it will be futile, for the angels themselves will not answer him. In verse 2 the word "vexation" applies to Job; it means literally "impatience," an attitude which Eliphaz can detect in him. Such impatience and passion ("jealousy") will bring down on Job the righteous judgment of God. Eliphaz has seen things work out this way; he has seen the "fool" apparently prospering but soon being destroyed. "I cursed his dwelling" is an elliptical way of saying "I saw that his dwelling was cursed" or "I regarded his dwelling as cursed."

From this point on Eliphaz is concerned with drawing a picture of God's judgment on the "fool," or wicked man, with primary emphasis on the tragic results for the rising generation. The words have a barbed reference to Job's own case, for his own sons were "crushed," and there was "no one to deliver them." The last part of verse 5 is difficult to translate; but the thought deals with the failure of the wicked to keep their possessions.

Eliphaz repeats his basic contention (from 4:8) that affliction and trouble are not accidental. They do not just happen, spring-ing up, as it were, from the dust. Man himself "begets" trouble. This translation, following the Greek version, is better than "is born to trouble." It is inevitable that man makes his own dis-tresses, as inevitable as that sparks fly upward. Job's tragedy, then, must have its root cause in himself.

Your Own Future Is Secure (5:8-27)

The solution which Eliphaz proposes is indeed simple, but it has little bearing on Job's particular situation. To "seek God" and to "commit" his cause to God is precisely what Job wanted to do. But to Eliphaz this would mean a kind of submissive, pa-tient trustfulness which was impossible for Job, since it involved trust in a deity of whose benevolent character Job was by no means sure. Verses 9 and 10 are a kind of doxology, in praise of the power of God. Such doxologies appear frequently in the book (see, for example, 22:12-14; 26:7-13; 36:24-33). The power of God as described by Eliphaz operates in the realm of nature (vs. 10) and in the realm of morals (vss. 11-16). It is God who so moves human affairs that the lowly are exalted and the "crafty" are frustrated. The first part of verse 13 is quoted by Paul in I Corinthians 3:19, the only direct quotation from the Book of Job in the New Testament. For Eliphaz it was a statement of God's moral governance of the world; for Paul it applied especially to the futility of all human wisdom or "craftiness" in the light of the true wisdom in Jesus Christ. Eliphaz sees the wicked unable to achieve their plans (for a parallel to verse 14 see Isa. 59:10), and he draws the dogmatic conclusion that the "poor [usually, the righteous] have hope, and injustice shuts her mouth."

In the conclusion of his speech Eliphaz turns to the contrasting side of God's providential rule. Just as the wicked come to ruin and frustration, so the righteous must come to eventual prosperity and peace. Without making a pointed charge that Job has sinned, he counsels submission to the purpose of God in this personal tragedy. Eliphaz regards the experience as a corrective and puri-fying process, a point which Elihu later makes in greater detail (33:19-28). Job is actually to be considered "happy," in line with the dogmatic assumption that all suffering was from the hand of God and designed for good purposes (see Prov. 3:11-12, a part of which Eliphaz restates here). The truth in such a view was never more beautifully put than by Eliphaz in verses 18-26. The reference to "six troubles" and "seven" recalls a similar use of numbers in Proverbs 6:16; 30:29; and in Amos 1:3.

By the time Eliphaz reaches his climax it is again evident that he has lost all sense of the actualities of Job's case. To say that in the end Job would be able to inspect his sheepfold and find nothing missing, that his descendants would be many, and that he would come to his grave "in ripe old age" was to intensify the pain already felt by a man in the prime of life facing death, with his children destroyed and his possessions gone. That it did actually so work out does not alter the situation. Here as elsewhere Eliphaz was not speaking "what is right" (42:7). His confident and indeed arrogant conclusion (vs. 27) does not comfort Job but increases his irritation.

What are we to make of this speech in view of its strange mixture of truth and error? The simplest thing is to say that it is true in general; its error lies in the attempt to deal with the practical case. Many of the things Eliphaz says can be substantiated elsewhere in Scripture; upon this same position intelligent faith rests. But although his words are true, they do not fit every situation. Eliphaz' theology was too small. It could not deal with a terrible calamity in any other terms than the most general assertions.

Job Speaks (6:1—7:21)

Such Advice Does No Good (6:1-27)

Eliphaz has expressed his settled conviction, based on experience, that "vexation," or impatience, kills the fool (5:2), warning that Job had symptoms of such fatal impatience. Now Job speaks and defends his attitude. If his impatience, or his calamity which gives rise to it, were weighed, it would prove to be so heavy that it would account for his rash words.

Moreover, in answer to Eliphaz' superficial advice to "seek God" Job declares that God is his *antagonist*. Job's disease and troubles are the arrows of God, poisoned arrows, against which there is no defense.

Verse 5 is Job's repeated justification of his exaggerated language. The very fact that he protests is proof that he has no satisfaction to keep him quiet. The following two verses obviously refer to something insipid, either the advice of Eliphaz which Job refuses to swallow, or, more probably, the flat and tasteless existence to which Job is doomed. He can find nothing in which to be confident or upon which to base hope.

He comes back, therefore, to his original plea—that he be allowed to die (vss. 8-9). Then he would have at least one slight consolation, enabling him to bear pain—that he had not yielded to the natural temptation (and the advice of his wife, if the Prologue is yet in view) and forsaken God. Death would be more than welcome if, in addition to relief from his pains and his despair, it would deliver him from the danger of such a denial.

Once again Job reminds his friends of the true situation. It is useless to counsel him to trust and to wait. He has neither the strength for waiting nor a future for which to wait. He is utterly without resource or help save in the friends themselves. His disappointment in them shows in verses 14-23, where he compares them to promising streams which run dry at the very time they are needed.

The Revised Standard Version rendering of verse 14 makes very good sense out of a difficult verse, although the thought is surprising. It represents a high spiritual standard in its implication that not merely unkind action, but indeed failure to perform the most elementary acts of kindness (for "a friend"), is to depart from true religion ("the fear of the Almighty").

After the extended picture of the dry beds of streams which traveling caravans seek in vain, Job declares that this is what the friends have become for him. Their fright at the enormity of his distress has paralyzed them, so that they cannot offer any help beyond the most superficial words. In sarcasm he asks a number of questions which point to the fact that he had not solicited their aid, certainly not the kind of aid Eliphaz offered. He could stand sound advice, even if it would point realistically to some error sufficient to explain his tragedy (vs. 24). But the kind of empty reproof they give ignores his despair and shows that they lack even the fundamentals of human sympathy (vs. 27).

I Have No Future at All (6:28—7:6)

Job has just called into question not only the truth of Eliphaz' words but even the motives of the friends (vs. 27). The next section opens with an appeal to them to "look" at him and to "turn." "My vindication," he says, "is in the matter; it is the point at issue." It is as though he were saying, "Stick to the facts in the

case." That his presentation is true is stressed by the first line of
verse 30, and the second line insists that he is perfectly capable
of discerning a calamity when it happens.

The calamity which he begs the friends to consider is vividly
described in 7:1-6. Job begins with a statement of the generally
difficult and unsatisfying lot of men on earth. Man is compared
to a soldier (the "hard service" is usually that of a mercenary
soldier) and to a hired servant. Life itself does not accord with
Eliphaz' rosy picture. As for Job, he, in common with humanity,
is like a slave looking for the respite that evening will bring. But
his case is even worse than the lot of man in general. In the place
of days of hard labor he has *months* of emptiness, with no reward
or wages; and the night which gives rest to the slave brings him
only increased pain. The contrast rises to a bitter climax in verse
4, where he reflects on the fact that, unlike the rest of hardwork-
ing mankind, for him the very length of the night is a horror, not
a blessing. Verse 5 is a graphic description of his disease which
gives no prospect of release. Finally, although he longs for death,
he also bewails the fact that life is short at best; it passes with the
swiftness of a shuttle crossing the loom; and, at least in his case,
it passes without a ray of hope.

Therefore I Complain to God (7:7-21)

In an abrupt change of direction, occasioned by verse 6 with
its pessimistic conclusion, Job now turns to God himself. One of
the most prominent features in this book is the way that Job, time
and again, in very depths of his despair, does turn to God. This
is all the more significant when we are reminded that in his view
God is his antagonist, that his tragedy has come from the hand of
God, and that he cannot be at all sure that God even hears, much
less cares. Even so, he addresses him, the Unseen, the Author of
his distresses. And he addresses him in the main as Friend. True,
it is as One who *has been* a Friend and who is now unaccountably
estranged. But still, through all of his agonized protest, there runs
the perception that God cannot be entirely against him.

In verse 7 the verb "remember" is in the singular, in contrast
with the preceding verbs where Job speaks directly to the friends
(for example, 6:28). Here it is clear that Job is speaking to God,
or at least is crying out in the direction of God. It is God who is
called upon to remember that Job's life is short and hopeless and
that in a "breath" he will be gone. In the very moment that God's

eye is upon him—and note that Job somehow recognizes that God's eye *is* upon him—Job will die.

Death, which will bring the desired release from pain, will nevertheless mean that communion with God and vindication are now impossible. Sheol will be the end. Man does not return from there; even God does not come there. (For another picture of Sheol see 3:13-19.) For Job there is as yet no hope of vindication in an afterlife. The hopelessness with which man must face the future without some new revealing by God, especially without the resurrection of Jesus Christ, was never more poignantly expressed than in verses 9 and 10. Here, in its emptiness, the Book of Job points to the New Testament for "fulfillment."

Since the future is without hope, Job justifies (vs. 11) the extravagance of his past language and the even more violent protest to come. His question, "Am I the sea?" is, of course, addressed to God. It recalls the common view that the sea was a symbol of cosmic evil and was forcibly restrained by God from breaking out so as to destroy the established order.

In verses 13-16 he returns to a description of his disease and its accompanying mental distress, including nightmares and a settled desire for death. "Rather than my bones" is a reference to his emaciated body. In verse 16 he vacillates between longing for death and longing for temporary relief.

Psalm 8, with its question, "What is man that thou art mindful of him . . . ?" (Ps. 8:4) is a great poem praising God's provision for man and wondering at the exalted position which man holds in God's creation. Job 7:17-18 is a deliberate parody of the thought of the Psalm, as Job complains about the constant attentiveness of God and marvels that God gives such minute concern to man as to visit him with pain and to try him "every moment."

There follows a series of ironic questions, betraying Job's agony, but also showing that he shared to some extent Eliphaz' view of a remote God. First, he asks how long he must be tormented by God. "Till I swallow my spittle" is apparently a proverbial expression, referring to a brief time. Next he poses the hypothetical case: Even granted that he has sinned (which he does not admit), of what concern is it to God? That he can ask such a question shows that he does not comprehend either the enormity of sin or the true nature of a God of holy love. To sin is indeed to "do" something to God, something so great that a Cross is necessary to deal with it.

But if this flaw appears in Job's theology, there is also the other, stronger strain of implicit faith. The questions which continue in verses 20 and 21, with their repeated "why's," emphasize not just Job's search for meaning in his tragedy, but more especially his pathetic loneliness and his longing for God. This comes to sharpest expression in the last verse, which repeats the fact that he is very near death. He will die, but God will ultimately "seek" him. This conviction that God is one who must finally seek man, who cannot be forever estranged from man, is evidence of the spiritual strength of Job. It is also a powerful witness to the true nature of God made fully known in Jesus Christ, who *is* God's search for man. In Job's case, however, this search will be fruitless, for Job "shall not be." Like a child after punishment, he cries, "I will die, and you will be sorry." Such a cry, although Job does not recognize it, can be addressed only to one whose nature it is to love.

Bildad Speaks (8:1-22)

Justice Will Be Done (8:1-7)

A comparison of Bildad's opening words (8:2) with those of Eliphaz (4:2) shows a real progression. Where Eliphaz is gentle and considerate Bildad is abrupt and harsh. It may be that the author wished to indicate in this way an actual character differentiation in the two men. Or it may be that he thus indicated a rising intensity in the discussion. Job's words in chapters 6 and 7 have been more and more violent, and the friends, who are fast being transformed into opponents, are shocked into sterner protest and into a more realistic appraisal of the situation.

They have hitherto assumed that Job was righteous and that the reverses he had suffered were only temporary and relatively unimportant. Now they begin to look for an alternate solution. This is suggested by Bildad's questions (vs. 3) and by his two hypotheses (vss. 4 and 6). The questions deal with the fact that in Bildad's view Job has actually charged God with injustice. Any reasonable theology, of course, must assert the opposite. Job had not, in fact, so charged God, although the drift of his protest was in this direction precisely because he was unable to reconcile his own case with a reasonable theology.

The hypotheses are negative and positive. The first (vs. 4)

reasons that the catastrophic death of Job's children could be an exact illustration of the working of a law of rewards and retribution. It could be, Bildad guesses, with a callous indifference to Job's parental grief, that the children had sinned and were punished. It should be noted that in his view they would have been punished, not directly by God, but by their own transgression, conceived of as an inexorable force, working its own retribution.

On the other side, if Job were, or were to become, pure and upright, then God would "rouse himself" for him. The result would be the usual happiness and prosperity.

Especially evident in Bildad's speech is the fact that in both instances the results are almost entirely mechanical. Sin punishes the wrongdoer; in much the same way righteousness on the part of man arouses God's concern and sets in motion the train of circumstances which leads to a happy conclusion. It is this mechanical view of life, and of God himself, which is challenged by the Book of Job.

It Has Always Been So (8:8-19)

In harmony with his formal, lifeless theology, Bildad gives the basis for such a view. It should not be surprising to learn that it is based on tradition, blindly and indiscriminately followed. The "fathers" are cited by Bildad (vss. 8-10). In view of man's brief life, so brief that wisdom cannot be achieved, it is necessary to rest upon what former generations have found, even though their wisdom has as little to do with present concerns as Bildad's advice has to do with Job's situation.

In verses 11-19 a series of images supports the basic contention of Bildad that the wicked man is insecure and his prosperity transient. An even stronger statement of the same principle appears in Bildad's second speech (ch. 18). There the matter is explored in frightening detail; here the treatment is more suggestive. The central images are the water reed, the spider's web, and the plant growing on rocky ground. The first recalls Egypt, where the papyrus plant grows luxuriantly on the banks of the Nile. Verse 11 seems at first reading to be a kind of cause-and-effect argument, but it anticipates verse 12, where the point is established that although such plants make rapid growth they quickly wither when water is removed. The same temporary and ephemeral character of the security of evil men is symbolized in verses 14 and 15 where that security is likened to a spider's web; it breaks down even while the man leans in confidence against it. Finally, such men are likened to a plant growing rapidly under the warm sun but on insufficient ground, so that it is quickly destroyed and forgotten (vs. 18). The same figure appears in Matthew 13:5-6 where, however, the heat of the sun is the force of destruction. The reference to "joy" in verse 19 is certainly ironic.

This Should Be Your Confidence (8:20-22)

Bildad concludes with a repetition of the hope which Eliphaz held out (5:17-27). His statement is briefer than that of Eliphaz, but it has the same note of assurance. It is evident also that his temper has somewhat subsided.

Job Speaks (9:1—10:22)

But I Cannot Reach God (9:1-20)

As was noted in the Introduction, the speakers in the discussion usually do not address themselves directly to the questions raised by the immediately preceding speaker. Sometimes they move in entirely new directions, sometimes they speak to a point raised several speeches before. Job's speech here begins with a consideration of major issues in the speeches of both Eliphaz and Bildad. In 4:17 Eliphaz has asked, "Can mortal man be righteous before God?" Bildad in 8:3 has asked, "Does God pervert justice? Or does the Almighty pervert the right?" Job's "I know that it is so" may be taken as agreement with the truth in these fundamental points. No man is absolutely pure in relation to God, and God does not twist justice. But Job's question is not answered by either truth. That question is: How can a man, a frail human being, establish his own *relative* justice before God? How can his righteousness be argued, or even presented as a case?

Job proceeds to a statement of the massive power of God, so complete that man has no handhold on him, no point at which to approach him. If one wished to enter a legal suit with God ("contend," vs. 3) he would find it impossible. The contest would be too unequal if it involved the God who causes earthquakes (vss. 5-6), who controls the forces of nature (vss. 7-8), and whose works are marvelous beyond understanding (vss. 9-10). This catalogue of evidences of God's power has parallels to other doxologies in the book (see, for example, 5:9-11 and comment), and it is, in fact, somewhat like the great closing speeches of the Lord himself (chs. 38-41). Here, however, the whole point is that the God of such power is really unapproachable. The climactic expression of his power is in verse 12: when God snatches no one can stay him, and no one can even question him. But it must be noted that Job is now presenting the popular attitude and not his own. The answer to the question "Who will say to him, 'What doest thou'?" is of course, "Job!" He is doing just that—questioning the purpose of God. His determination, moreover, is to force the question where it can find a proper answer—in the presence of God himself.

In the following verses Job comes back to the impossibility of his task. Verse 13 in the Revised Standard Version means that God is set in anger against Job. It is possible, however, to understand in the first line "a god" rather than "God." In this case the reference would be to the old view of creation, where God overcame the forces of chaos and conquered the primeval monster. Even "a god" could not divert the Lord, since even the "helpers of Rahab" yielded to him at creation. (See the comment at 3:8. The poet's use of the language of ancient mythologies does not mean that he accepted the thought of these mythologies. It is evident that the author of the Book of Job was a strict monotheist.)

If even "a god" would be powerless before God, Job would have no chance of answering a charge made by him. His dilemma is that the condemned must appeal, not to an impartial judge, but to the very one who has caused his misery (vs. 15). So far has Job's skepticism advanced in his own relationship with God, that now he would not be able to credit it even if God were to answer him (vs. 16). This skepticism is evident also in his bitter exclamations in verses 19 and 20. God can best him in any contest, so that before such a judge even his protestation of innocence would become evidence of guilt.

God's Actions Seem to Be Indiscriminate (9:21-24)

Job has just given expression to almost complete skepticism about his personal relationship to God (vss. 13-20). Now he expresses an even more serious skepticism about God's governance of the world. In anticipation of the fact that his words will skirt out-and-out blasphemy, he begins (vs. 21) with an avowal that he is not concerned with saving his life, at least not at the expense of truth. The truth, as he sees it in verses 22-24, is that there is no difference in the lot of the righteous and that of the wicked. This is not the simple statement that good and bad alike die (as Eccles. 9:2) but the charge that destruction, or calamity, overtakes them both without discrimination. Moreover, God himself mocks the calamity of the innocent. Finally, instead of establishing justice, God supports wickedness.

The charge ends with the pointed question: "If it is not he, who then is it?" And everyone must echo, "Who, indeed?" Job's view of life is as extreme and as false in its exaggeration as that of the friends. But it has one advantage which theirs lacks: it takes evil seriously. It takes it so seriously, in fact, that faith in God is imperiled; but it is honest. To the author it was apparently not sufficient to answer the question in the way of the Prologue, "It is Satan!" Job's question must stand—either until God gives it answer or until the force of evil is somehow blunted.

There Is No Arbiter Between Us (9:25-35)

In verses 25-26 there are three moving images of the brevity of life and of the swiftness with which Job's own life is coming to an end without resolution of his problem. He cannot by any means put that problem aside, either by forgetting it or by minimizing it (vss. 27-28). His whole prospect is despairing, for even though he were to establish his innocence, washing in snow water and lye, such innocence would not affect the God who plagued him so.

Verse 32 has often been cited as a remarkable anticipation of New Testament truth. It is clearly an indication that Job not only knew the exact nature of his problem but also knew that any solution, to be satisfactory, would have to be given on a level which man could understand, or at least accept. His complaint that God is not a man, so that the two of them might come together, points to the need for God's mightiest act of all when, in his Son, he did become man, so that he might bring us together to glory (see Heb. 2:10-18). Verse 33 points us in an even more direct way to the New Testament. If we read the first line, as in the margin, "Would that there were an umpire between us," we catch Job's desperate longing that there be One who could stand as an Arbiter between God and man, not merely to settle a dispute but even, by laying his hand on both, to bring them into complete reconciliation.

The last two verses of chapter 9 are difficult to understand. They are probably transitional, leading to the direct appeal to God which comes in chapter 10, and represent Job's disappointment that there was for him no such arbiter and that in himself there were no resources for meeting the crisis he faced.

Even So I Question His Purpose (10:1-22)

Job's answer to Bildad represents the extreme limit of his skepticism. Nowhere else does he go so far in outright challenge of God and in dispute of God's moral governance. But even in this violent outburst we can detect notes of unconscious faith, which are all the more important because they sound out in the midst of bleak despair. Thus in chapter 10 Job actually turns once again to God. True, he turns with ironic question and sarcastic tone, but it is to God, the God whom he has just charged with out-and-out indifference. As before (7:11-21) and later (for example, 14:13-17) he directs his words to the unseen Antagonist, his onetime Friend.

The transition from his answer to Bildad to his words to God is clearly indicated in 10:1-2a. From here on to the end of the chapter it is as though the friends were not present. Job's language is as private as a prayer—certainly not one of praise or trust, but still a prayer.

Job raises hypotheses which could conceivably explain his case. Since no one of them is argued seriously, it is evident that they are meant to be taken as inadequate or false explanations. The first, in verse 3, is the possibility that God is completely cruel, actually finding pleasure in inflicting pain. Another (vss. 4-5) is either that, like a man, God must take revenge swiftly and without regard to justice, or that God sees as imperfectly as men see, and hence does not really know what justice is.

In verse 8 Job turns to the paradoxical fact that he has not only been made by God (vss. 8-11) but has actually been the object of God's love and of such care that his life ("breath" rather than "spirit" in vs. 12) has been preserved. The figure of God as potter and man as clay is, of course, familiar in Scripture. The metaphors of birth in verses 10 and 11 are in keeping with primitive notions of procreation, although they may be only poetic images balancing the one in verse 9.

The other side of the paradox is the fact that, though expending such attention and care on Job, God had from the beginning been set in his purpose to destroy him (vs. 13). In Job's case it is all the same whether he has committed sins, or is a settled wicked man, or is righteous (vss. 14-15). As in 9:22-24 he charges the Judge of all the earth with indiscriminate action, here he charges his own Creator with an indiscriminate purpose.

Job reiterates the hopelessness of such a situation (vss. 16-17). If God be against him, who can be for him? How can he be helped? Finally, since he has been brought into this life, meaningless as it is, he begs for a brief surcease from pain, and especially for a brief respite from God's attentive persecution, so that he may take a little comfort before death brings him to Sheol, the land where even "light is as darkness."

Zophar Speaks (11:1-20)

You Are Getting Less Than You Deserve (11:1-6)

The tenor of Zophar's first speech is noticeably different from those of Eliphaz and Bildad. Again this may be due to the way the author conceived of the character of the man, but more likely it is a device to indicate the mounting tension of the discussion (compare 8:2). Zophar speaks in more direct and unambiguous terms than the other two, and does not hesitate to make the specific charge of Job's sinfulness.

In the same way the opening words are stronger than those of Eliphaz, and even those of Bildad. Zophar speaks of Job as a man "full of talk," or literally "a man of lips," intimating that his words are not sincere. He regards his speech as "babble" and, worse, a mockery of God. The definite charge appears at verse 4. The first half is not a direct quotation but a rough summary of the direction of Job's thought. The second half recalls Job's affirmations in 9:21 and 10:7. His claim to be "clean" is the mockery which Zophar attacks, for he, like the others, insists on carrying on the discussion solely in terms of man's *absolute* righteousness.

Job has expressed his longing to speak to God and so present his case, although he knows the difficulty of such an enterprise (9:3, 15, 16). Zophar in turn wishes that God would speak to Job, in which case Job would find out far more than he bargained for. Specifically he would learn the "secrets of wisdom" which, in Zophar's viewpoint, would not be some kind of esoteric knowledge but the catalogue of Job's sins which God alone knew. This becomes clear when Zophar brings his charge to its point in the last line of verse 6.

It Is Useless to Try to Understand God (11:7-12)

Implicit in Job's complaints was the desire to understand his own case and, indeed, the general purpose and action of God. That this is possible Zophar categorically denies. In a passage of great beauty and, it must be admitted, of fundamental truth, he dwells on the impossibility of man's knowing the "deep things of God" or "the limit of the Almighty." Zophar knows that a complete definition of God would be the end of God. In verse 10 there is a reminiscence of Job's words in 9:12. Where Job makes the remark in bitterness, as an example of the indiscriminate operations of God, Zophar quotes it with apparent approval as an example of God's unsearchable nature and power. That he is indiscriminate, however, he denies, for God "knows worthless men" and does not ignore iniquity.

The natural effect of such a view of God, if completely unmodified, would be to abrogate the search for wisdom of any kind and to retire into agnosticism, an effect which Zophar comes close to expressing in verse 12. The Hebrew here is difficult, but the Revised Standard Version is probably right in understanding this as a statement of the utter impossibility that a stupid man (Job) should ever attain wisdom (see also 12:3).

You Need to Set Your Heart Aright (11:13-20)

Where then is wisdom? In Zophar's theology it is simply in submission, even if it be submission to unreason, and in repentance, even if there be no known sin. He counsels Job to give up the search for knowledge of God and to give himself to practical amendment of his own ways. In common with the others (5: 17-27; 8:20-22), but with even greater beauty, Zophar describes the happy issue which will come to Job when he thus submits. Particularly noticeable are Zophar's promising words, "There is hope" (vs. 18). In 7:6 Job has denied that he has hope, and to that denial he will return in 14:7 and 17:15-16. In some sense Zophar's words are prophetic, although they are insufficiently grounded. He promised the right thing for the wrong reason. The only ground of hope for Job was God himself, but it could not be the absent and unknowable God of the friends.

In the end, in keeping with the generally intense flavor of his speech, Zophar warns Job of the alternative. The wicked have no way out, and their only "hope" is death.

Job Speaks (12:1—14:22)

Everyone Knows What You Know (12:1-12)

The speech of Job is partly answer and partly summary, as it completes the first round of the discussion. It begins with a sarcastic reference to the friends, and particularly to the speech of Zophar. "No doubt you are the people," Job says, in recognition of their claim to infallible knowledge. Zophar has declared (11:12) that it was highly unlikely that a stupid man (like Job) would "get understanding" (literally, "get a heart," for the heart was regarded as the seat of the intellect). Job indignantly replies that he already has a "heart" (vs. 3) and is at least the mental equal of his counselors.

Verse 4 is an appeal, made once again, for the friends to consider the true facts in the case, which are the meaningless contradictions of Job's life. He, the just and blameless man, is now the laughingstock, the symbol of forsakenness and even of God's judgment. Verse 5 seems to be a side reference to the attitude of the friends, as Job remarks on the way in which ease blinds men to the misfortune of others. The last line of the verse may be translated, "a blow for those whose feet slip," meaning that the friends' position of security impels them to join in the common practice of hitting a man when he is down. Verse 6 is a repetition of Job's basic contention (ch. 9) that wickedness is not punished by God, or that his actions are indiscriminate. The last line of the verse probably refers to idolatry.

Job further maintains that it is perfectly obvious that what has happened is the doing of the Lord, that it is not accidental. Whether he means his own calamity or the relative security of the wicked and the idolatrous (vs. 6) is not clear. At any rate, he regards it as a commonplace of knowledge, apparent in the very order of nature, and so not to be argued. The last part of verse 9 is a parallel to Isaiah 41:20, and includes the single use of the divine name, "Yahweh" (English, "LORD"), in the speeches themselves (see comment on ch. 28). Because of this it has sometimes been suggested that the entire section (vss. 7-12) is out of place here, and that in fact it sounds more like one of the friends than like Job. Such a view is supported by the difficulty of verse 12 as it stands, since it is hardly likely that Job would here admit the wisdom of his elder friends (see the remark of Eliphaz on their greater age in 15:10). But verse 12 may well be a sarcastic question, or, better, a quotation in preparation for the thought of verse 13. Thus Job would be parodying the claims of the friends and denying them any special wisdom.

I Also Know the Wisdom and Power of God (12:13-25)

In contrast to the kind of wisdom the friends claim (and which Job abhors) he asserts that with God alone are wisdom and power (vs. 13; although the word "God" does not appear, the pronoun is emphatic). This basic fact is then elaborated in a description of the working of God's power and the incomprehensibility of his wisdom. Detailed comment is not necessary here, as the illustrations cited are clear enough. God's mighty acts are seen, for example, in droughts and floods (vs. 15), in the overthrow of human authorities (vss. 17-19, 21), in the reversals of national fortunes (vs. 23), and even in God's penetration of and control of the realms of darkness and mystery (vs. 22).

This recital, with its overtones of actual submission to apparent unreasoning, and unreasonable, activity of God, is not to be taken as an indication that Job has reversed his position. As the following chapter makes clear, he is unchanged in the basic protest he would make. Here he simply attempts to establish a common ground with the friends, that the argument may proceed.

I Want to Defend Myself Before Him (13:1-19)

Job's protest appears again in 13:1-16, in even stronger terms than before. First (13:1-2) Job sums up what he has said, almost by way of introduction, in chapter 12. Then he states the real issue. There are few places in the entire book where this issue comes to the light as plainly as here. This may, in fact, be taken as a simple statement of the *general* problem of the book, as distinct from Job's individual problem. The imagery is that of a courtroom (in modern terms; in ancient times it would have been the city gate). Job, acknowledging the omnipotence and the omniscience of God, nevertheless wants to find a way to present what is indisputably an irrational exception to the general rule of God's working.

In verse 4 he again refuses the words of the friends. Since, in the preceding chapter, he has declared himself in agreement with them, this must refer not to the basic truths of God's power and wisdom but to the conclusions the friends drew from those truths. Their lies have to do not so much with their theology as with the application of that theology to life—or its nonapplication—and with their resolute refusal to consider the meaninglessness or seeming irrationality of Job's situation.

Continuing the image of a legal proceeding Job asks, with some sarcasm, if the friends will undertake to represent God, almost as attorneys for the defense (vss. 6-11). If so, then they must beware lest they show the slightest improper partiality, for God himself would punish them for it. Job still must have some sense of the absolute justice of God!

One of Job's sharpest condemnations of the friends comes in verse 12 (see also 13:4-5 and 6:14-27). It has been imagined by some commentators that in this attack we have another dramatic touch, as in 6:27, and its result. Here, it is supposed, the friends are represented as rising in shocked protest, all speaking at once. Job, however, waves them back to their seats and, in the next verse, demands silence. He then repeats the basic position (from 13:3) in stronger language.

There are two main problems in verses 14-19. The first is the meaning of the expression "I will take my flesh in my teeth" (vs. 14). The second half of the verse clearly refers to a courageous hazarding of life as a venture (for the same expression see Judges 12:3; I Sam. 19:5). The first line, then, must be a parallel statement of the same attitude, but the figure is obscure. It may be, of course, a type of proverbial expression, the exact image of which is lost.

The other problem has to do with verse 15. Although the familiar rendering, "Though he slay me, yet will I trust in him," has a satisfactory ring to it, it cannot be derived from the Hebrew, and moreover, it does not fit the mood of Job. He has just stated his lack of concern for personal safety. He now faces the worst, namely, that he is dying at the hand of God. His position is precisely: "I have no hope" (see also 7:6; 11:18; 14:7; 17:15-16). He discards the possibility of hope *in this life,* and it is that honest appraisal, with all its reason for despair, that opens the door for the great advance he will later make when hope is found *beyond this life.* This magnificent movement of thought and experience is lost if the reading of the Revised Standard Version is not followed here.

Since Job has no hope, it is imperative that he prepare and state the full case without delay. It is also imperative that he do so without accepting the friends' charge of sin. He knows that in such a case only true godliness will stand (vs. 16).

The legal atmosphere is strongly present in verses 17-19. Here Job strikingly resembles a complainant who must plead his own case without outside aid. His confident assertion, "I know that I shall be vindicated," does not necessarily, at this point, mean that he will himself live to see such vindication. Rather, he is sure of the vindication itself which will come, even after death. The case will ultimately be decided for him, although he will not see it through. Verse 19 continues the thought; the question in the first line challenges either God or man to bring whatever evidence can be cited against him, for death is rapidly approaching (line 2).

Why Can I Not Reach Him in Life? (13:20—14:6)

It is characteristic of the discussion that when Job reaches a climax in his protestation he turns directly to God (see 7:12; 10:2). Here again, without any transitional words, he addresses himself to the God whom he must necessarily regard as the author of his difficulty. And again, even in the depth of his uncertainty, he addresses him as still his Friend. He asks two gifts: relief from his suffering, and release from the paralyzing dread of God that would naturally hinder a man from presenting the kind· of case he is outlining (vss. 20-21). The ideal situation for which he yearns is stated in verse 22—a situation in which God would speak clearly and unequivocally and Job would be able to marshal his arguments in defense, or where Job would present his complaint and God would give satisfactory reasons.

Since such firsthand meeting is not forthcoming, Job again hazards some guesses. Although some interpreters see in verse 23 a break in Job's confident assertions of integrity, it seems more probable in the light of this whole speech that the question is asked as a pure hypothesis—as though to say, "If *sin* is the explanation, why not point out *what* sins, since up to now none has been named." In the same way verse 26 is not to be taken as an admission that what Job now suffers is the direct result of sins committed in his early youth; it is another hypothesis which he advances as a possible but unproved reason for the catastrophe.

All of the contradictions and meaninglessness of Job's life are caught up in the pathetic words of verses 24-25 and 27. The word "enemy" in the original is a bitter wordplay on the name "Job." The descriptive images of the "driven leaf" and the "dry chaff" not only are pictures of his existence, but they also point up the sheer irrationality of the situation, where a man reduced to this frail state is *still* subjected to unceasing attention from God (vs. 27).

The thought of Job's frailty and the tenuous nature of his life suggests the fact that all life, even at its best, is transient and ephemeral. In a short but exceedingly moving section (13:28—14:6) Job dwells upon this basic paradox of man's existence (see also 7:1-2, 17). Verse 28 is difficult, for, as the margin indicates, the subject changes abruptly to the third person pronoun, although an antecedent does not appear until the following verse ("man"). For this reason some commentators have suggested that the verse is out of place and would come better after 14:6. It is possible that the original order was as it now appears, although it makes for disconnected thought.

The images in this section depict the brevity of man's life: "a rotten thing," a "moth-eaten" garment, "a flower," "a shadow." All substantiate the fundamental point that it is the nature of man's life to be short and full of trouble. The mystery is that God adds to this general misery by such special visitations as Job illustrates. Why, Job asks, need there be more suffering and fewer years than would be his common lot as "man . . . born of a woman"?

The question in verse 4 is hard to understand, for it breaks into the general theme of the brevity of man's life with a query about sin. Is Job agreeing that man is generally sinful? Or is he questioning the proposal that will be made a bit later, that tragedy is God's means of refining human life? (see 33:19-28). It seems fairly certain that he is at least giving assent to the truth that *in comparison with God* man is always "unclean" and no amount of experience will make him otherwise. Man will always be man, not God. But that truth does not alter the fact that Job's case is so special and his suffering so extraordinary that no explanation can be found in the ordinary constitution of man's life.

The section ends with a sad plea that God, who has set man within such a severely circumscribed life, give man peace in his limited days, to find what little joy he can (see also 7:19; 10:20).

Is There to Be Another Life? (14:7-22)

As Job's speech nears its conclusion it is clear that the author
has been working toward a great climax. Beginning with the contradictions of Job's own life, he turns next to the brevity of life in
general. Then the next stage is reached when the thought centers
on the fact of death itself as the great symbol both of Job's extreme dilemma and of the transitoriness of man's life. In 14:2
man has been compared to a flower, withering almost as soon as
it blooms. In 14:7 man is *contrasted* with a tree, as Job declares
that unlike man, nature shows some faint hope of survival beyond
what seems to be death.

The image is clear enough without explanation, as the contrast
is drawn between man's life and that of a felled tree. The tree
may "come back to life" but man dies and that is the end, final
and complete. There is no place in the Old Testament where the
common expectation and the common lack of hope are more
powerfully set forth than here. Job insists, against all suppositions
to the contrary, that death is the end, that Sheol rather than life
is man's final destiny (on "Sheol" see 3:11-19). That he makes
the point with such strong insistence may indicate that the book
was written at a time when the possibility of an afterlife was the
subject of popular discussion.

At verse 13 a remarkable change occurs. Job has been dwelling
upon the "Nevermore" placed by death over against man's life.
This death will be a "sleep" in Sheol. But suddenly a new possibility breaks in. Suppose there were something *beyond* Sheol!
Suppose Sheol were for him a time of waiting, so that beyond its
limits God would call him into renewed meeting. This possibility
raises the fascinating question in verse 14. It *is* a question for Job,
not an affirmation, but it is extraordinary, given the facts in his
case, that the thought should occur at all.

It is evident that the *only* basis for the possibility is Job's
knowledge of God and the prior fellowship with God which he
had enjoyed. Neither nature nor his own situation, nor even the
word of God in times past, gave Job reason to believe. Here is a
man who is thrown back entirely on God, but who, out of his
knowledge of God, comes to the conclusion that it is possible that
relationship with God is not to be ended by death.

This is not Job's greatest moment, but light is beginning to
break. It does not come in full flood yet—in fact, not until the

resurrection of Christ is the light seen in its fullness—but it is dawning here. All of Job's expressions about this possibility point to the personal character of his thought, as he dreams of God's calling him in love and drawing him into an appointed meeting.

Verses 16 and 17 admit of two possible interpretations. In the Revised Standard Version they are made to be a continuation of Job's passionate imagining of what it would be like to meet God beyond Sheol. Thus part of this meeting would be full and complete forgiveness. It must be admitted, however, that as yet Job has not accepted the fact that any such sins or iniquities need pardon. It is possible that the verses are to be taken in the opposite sense, and are a vivid self-reminder of the actualities of the present in contrast with the kind of future of which Job has been dreaming.

That the second interpretation is the more likely is indicated by verses 18-22, where the mood is quite pessimistic. After Job's hypothetical question he comes back to the realities of nature and of his own life. Although nature gives a faint hint of hope (14:7) it gives more evidence of final dissolution. Mountains crumble, even rocks are worn away, and similarly the "hope" of man is no solid, lasting hope. In the end Job comes back to the original conclusion which he had reached in 14:10-12. He can expect only death and beyond that nothing. Finally he takes a look at a possible solution, often proposed, that man has a real future in the generations that are to follow him. In brief contempt Job demolishes this as a false hope with no meaning for a man in deep tragedy. If succeeding generations are to be happy, it will bring the sufferer no release. Men do not know or profit from the experiences of their children; they know only the pains of their own existence (for a stronger statement of the same thought see 21:19-21).

THE SECOND ROUND OF DISCUSSION
Job 15:1—21:34

Eliphaz Speaks (15:1-35)

Your Attitude Is Irreverent (15:1-6)

One of the evident structural features of the Book of Job is a marked difference in the leading themes of the three stages of discussion. In keeping with the general freedom of the book these themes are not followed slavishly, and they always allow some room for much variety and many auxiliary ideas. There can be little doubt, however, that in the first round of speeches (chs. 3-14) the author meant to call attention to Job's case as an exception to the generally accepted view that righteousness is rewarded. In the second cycle the theme shifts. The atmosphere becomes darker, the speeches of the friends more acrimonious, and the situation more tense. The theme now is the ultimate fate of the wicked. The friends are represented as following through their suspicion that Job is not an exception to the general rule but is in fact an illustration of its inflexible working, an example of the fact that the wicked are always visited with punitive suffering.

As he did in his first speech (4:2-6), so here Eliphaz begins with at least the appearance of hesitation and a justification of what must be said. He appears to be debating with himself, asking whether answering Job will be worth the effort (vss. 2-3). That he does speak is explained by the fact that to him Job's attitude and words were actually destructive of religion. The phrase "fear of God" (vs. 4) is virtually equivalent to "reverence" or even "religion." It is often the case that honestly spoken expressions of actual doubt are taken as dangerous blaspheming. Nothing could be farther from the truth than that Job was destroying either faith or "meditation," but to those whose faith was perhaps none too secure, his daring challenge of God could seem to do so. At any rate, Eliphaz does not hesitate to call Job's words the product of "iniquity" and to say that Job stands condemned by what he has said (vs. 6).

Your Demand Is Impossible (15:7-16)

Sarcasm, which plays a considerable part in this book, appears again when Eliphaz asks if Job imagines that he is "the first man." The reference, of course, is to Adam who might be supposed to have had some immediate, firsthand knowledge of God. Eliphaz asks if Job thinks that he has, or can have, the very wisdom of God. In the Book of Proverbs "wisdom" speaks saying, "Before the hills, I was brought forth" (Prov. 8:25). Job, in his search, is squarely in line with the thought of the writer of Proverbs 8 and 9, who believed that the wisdom of God, by which—or by *whom*—the world was brought into being, resided also in the mind of man (see Prov. 8:15-16, 31). But to Eliphaz such an assumption is incredible; to him the way of "wisdom" would be to retire from the effort to understand, and to give up asking the kind of apparently arrogant questions Job asks.

Or, the way of wisdom would be to submit to the recommendations of the friends, who represent the accumulated wisdom of the past. Eliphaz defends the right of the friends to speak and the validity of their advice (vss. 9-11), reminding Job that they have the advantage of age (Job, it must be remembered, was not an old man), and that they represent the very words of God for Job. Eliphaz does not lack self-sufficiency when he identifies himself and the others as "the consolations of God." He also betrays his complete indifference to the dimensions of Job's provocation when he asks in surprise, "Why do you talk this way?" (see vss. 12-13).

In verse 14 Eliphaz apparently refers to Job's assertion in 14:4, although it is also a repetition of his own thought in 4:17-18. Both men, then, agree that *in comparison with God* no man can be accounted clean or righteous. But they differ in their conclusions. Job insists that the question is not man's righteousness in comparison with God's, but his own righteousness as a man living under the demands of God. (He might have pointed out that if the question were man's absolute cleanness, then Eliphaz himself would stand, like the rest of mankind, under judgment.) Eliphaz draws a different conclusion: that since absolute righteousness is impossible, it is futile to attempt to establish *relative* righteousness or to question the assumption that suffering is punitive.

A Wicked Man Is Destined for Distress (15:17-35)

The definition of the wicked man's destiny which comes in verses 20-35 is introduced by the solemn declaration that this is no new and foreign doctrine, but is the truth of the past which has been handed down in pure form from the time of the fathers. No "stranger" has formed it—a gratuitous intimation that Job's views are not only unorthodox, they are positively alien.

It has been pointed out that at times the three friends seem literally to turn their backs on Job as they set forth their predetermined conclusions about his case, as though they do not wish to be confused by the facts (see 5:17-27). Here Eliphaz goes a step further and turns his back on life itself, declaring the absolute truth of principles that are plainly contradicted by life. This is another place where the words of the Book of Job are not to be taken as literally or universally true. Even the most superficial acquaintance with life affords illustrations of the fact that the wicked man does *not* writhe "in pain all his days" (vs. 20).

It is worthwhile to reflect on what *is* true here, and it must be noted that as a statement of the emptiness of the wicked life and the futility of an arrogant attempt to contravert the will of God this is profoundly true. It is true, moreover, that the wicked is "destined for the sword," and that defiance of God is the way of ultimate defeat (vss. 22, 25-26).

In verses 27-30 Eliphaz describes the pride of the wicked man ("fatness" is a symbol of arrogance and pride), his heedlessness (as he inhabits places which God has plainly marked out as fit only for destroying judgment), and the certainty of his unprofitable end. The latter thought is extended in verses 31-35, where a series of images points up the precarious character of the life of the "godless" and his lack of any future save barrenness and destruction.

Job Speaks (16:1—17:16)

You Are Miserable Comforters (16:1-5)

Job begins again, as he has before (12:2-3), with a personal gibe at the friends, calling them "miserable comforters" (a possible reference to Eliphaz' claim in 15:11 that they are "the consolations of God"). Eliphaz has charged Job with speaking "windy knowledge" (15:2); Job replies that he has no right to expect the "wind" to stop, and that Eliphaz is not obligated to answer. He asserts that, if their situations were reversed, Job would be quite a different kind of "comforter": instead of such unfeeling criticisms as theirs, he would give solace and comfort for their pain (vs. 5b).

My Distress Is Terrible (16:6-17)

Verse 6 brings the subject back to Job's case, to his own pain which, far from being assuaged, is unremitting. Moreover, in plain words he declares that the responsibility must actually be placed on God. Each of the details of his tragedy he must identify as the direct activity of God. Thus it is God who has "worn" him out and who has alienated him from his friends (vs. 7); it is God who has made his sufferings a "witness" against him (vs. 8);

it is God, in short, who is his adversary (vs. 9; the image is that of a dangerous beast). Verses 10 and 11 show that involved in Job's agony is the fact that he has become a symbol of God's curse, thereby becoming alienated from men, who do not hesitate to treat him with contempt (see also 17:6).

Job then returns to the list of his grievances as he recites the ways in which God has mistreated him (vss. 12-16). Here the images are those of an archer pursuing his prey and an army taking a city or fortress. As he reaches a climax he describes the way he has come to unrelieved mourning, having laid his "strength" (literally, "horn," a symbol of pride and exaltation) in the dust. Finally (vs. 17) he repeats his basic position that the explanation for this frightful tragedy cannot be found in any supposed wickedness on his part.

Where Is There One on My Side? (16:18-22)

Job's speeches frequently show shifts from the depths of despair to startling reaches of faith (for example, 14:1-6 and 14:7-17; 19:2-22 and 19:23-27) and from faith to despair (for example, 14:7-17 and 14:18-22; 23:10-12 and 23:13-17). Verses 18-22 represent such a venture of faith, not a complete confidence but a venture in the direction from which help must finally come. First Job, the wronged sufferer, the object of God's anger—as he must think—appeals to the earth itself to be his witness. He is facing a death which he is compelled to interpret as judicial murder. Vindication can come only if the ground itself will take up the cry of "Injustice!" The imagery is the same as that in Genesis 4:10 where the "voice" of Abel's blood cries out from the ground in testimony against Cain. But even this kind of dramatic witness to the essential rightness of his complaint is not enough to satisfy Job. He knows that there is needed a vocal, personal witness and he affirms his conviction that this witness is in heaven. "Witness" means, of course, not simply one who gives factual testimony, but one who stands *for* the accused in a trial, a kind of "advocate." Job makes his faith plain when he declares that the one who will vouch for him is "on high" (vs. 19). Does he think of God himself as this "Witness" for the defense and not really the Enemy he has just called him? Or does he think of God as somehow *both* Adversary and Advocate, both against and for Job? Or does he think of another one, one in distinction from God, one who pleads Job's case before God? In the light of the context the first seems improbable. Job has already suggested a kind of contradiction in the dealing if not the nature of God, and later he will elaborate the idea (17:3), although ultimately it is discarded as a solution. This may be as far as Job can go at this stage, that is to affirm that, despite the plain evidence to the contrary—evidence he cannot disregard for it pertains to his own real sufferings—God must be somehow *for* him. This is certainly the sense of his prayer in verse 21, that God would be—or would show himself to be—one who stands for man, like a man himself taking up the concerns of his neighbor. When we remember the Hebrew conception that responsibility for righting injustice rested upon the "near kinsman," we see how Job is being prepared for the leaping insight of 19:25. And in this section we see how the thought of the Book of Job points strongly to the New Testament, witnessing to the necessity and the nature of the Incarnation.

Verse 22 presents a special problem, for Job here speaks of death as coming within "a few years." Everywhere else in the book he views death as imminent, and everywhere else he contemptuously dismisses every suggestion of his friends that he has any time left in which to find his vindication. In the very next verse he speaks of his days as "extinct." Some interpreters understand here not "a few years" but "the number of years," meaning that the number of his years has been completed. This involves a slight change in the text as we have it, and it is not entirely satisfactory as a solution. It may be that we have here a poetic expression which points not to length but to brevity, or it may be that the original text has somehow become obscure.

Instead of Hope I Have Only Despair (17:1-16)

In chapter 17 Job is facing the prospect of immediate death. This he emphasizes in three dramatically broken outcries, bewailing his broken spirit, his extinct days, and the waiting grave (17:1). The movement of his thought parallels that of chapter 16 as he turns from the injustice of his situation to the failure of all human resources (17:2), finally back to God (vss. 3-5). Verse 3 is clearly an appeal to God, his Judge, to be his Witness or Advocate as well. In the concept of God's laying down a "pledge" with himself there appears again the thought of God who is *for* Job along with the God who is *against* him. The second line asks in desperation if there is anyone (besides God) who can give "surety" for Job, that is, who can stand for him.

Verse 4 in the Revised Standard Version involves a slight change in the text, and suggests that Job is certain his friends have no prospect of triumph over him in their arguments, for the same God who has visited Job with suffering has visited them with obtuseness. In the same mood verse 5 is a bitter thrust against the friends, likening them to informers for personal gain, and warning them that the results they may receive will be quite different from what they expect. It must be admitted that it is hard to see how this fits the thought of the section, and it is certainly extreme to charge Eliphaz, Bildad, and Zophar with taking a stand against Job because they hope to have a share in his property (according to the Prologue he had none left!). It is better to concede that in this verse we again have a text the meaning of which is not clear—no new view, for the ancient Greek version, the Septuagint, omits the first line of verse 5.

In verse 6 Job returns to the tragic circumstances of his life, dwelling on them with a kind of morbid fascination. God has made him a "byword" (for the same idea see 12:4) and a symbol of God's curse.

In verse 8 Job either points to his case as a present cause for wonder or, more probably, to the fact that he will in the future stand as an astonishment (the verbs may be read as futures). In the latter case he is expressing his confidence that in days to come he will not be a byword or an object of scorn, but a symbol for the righteous and a stimulus to the innocent to withstand the "godless." This may be the reason, then, that he makes the amazing assertion of verse 9, that in spite of all temptations, in spite of the proddings of his disease, in spite of the advice of the friends, he will hold fast to his claim of integrity and will thereby grow "stronger and stronger." It is certainly a surprising remark, representing another dramatic shift in the mood of the speaker. It is, moreover, the explanation of verse 10, where Job apparently has to call back his friends, who have risen to leave in shocked protest against such bold impiety.

The contrast between actuality and the superficial judgments of the friends appears vividly in the closing words of Job's speech, words of great pathos (vss. 11-16). They have declared that "night" is day; that is, they reverse the truth or treat what is undeniably dark as not dark at all. This is supported by the remark in the second line, where Job summarizes their advice as a kind of bland assertion that soon the darkness will be over, that morning is about to dawn for Job. The opposite is true, he declares, for his whole existence is now turned not to dawn but to darkness, to the darkness of death and Sheol. Who is he to hope as they have advised him? How can he hope? Do they mean that he is to carry his hope with him into Sheol?

Bildad Speaks (18:1-21)

Do You Expect a Miracle? (18:1-4)

The English translation of the opening words of Bildad's second speech does not make it clear whether the speaker addresses Job or speaks to a group (the pronoun "you" may be either singular or plural). The Hebrew here has the plural, the ancient Greek translation the singular. The singular fits better the general framework of the discussion, where the speakers normally speak in this fashion. If the plural is correct, then we must assume either that Bildad includes with Job some bystanders whom he understands to be siding with Job or that he addresses not only Job but also Eliphaz and Zophar, who have not given sufficiently strong arguments.

Bildad's question in verse 3 may be a reference to Job's sarcastic remark that even the "beasts" could teach the friends (12:7). Certainly his description of Job as one who tears himself in his anger recalls Job's contention that God "has torn" him (16:9). The basic question Bildad asks appears in verse 4: that is, whether Job really expects to achieve a complete reversal of the normal order of creation, for so Bildad understands the drift of Job's demands. To the friends, it would be equivalent to turning creation topsy-turvy to admit that suffering such as Job's could come upon the righteous, or that the wicked should escape unscathed.

The Wicked Man Has No Peace at All (18:5-21)

The remainder of Bildad's speech is a strong application of the orthodox principle of rewards and retribution, particularly as it affects the fate of wicked men. It is a picture full of dramatic imagery, tracing the way disaster comes upon the wicked man (vss. 5-7), the uneasiness of his entire life (vss. 8-11), the dreadful consequences of his downfall (vss. 12-14), the destruction of his posterity (vss. 15-17), and the final annihilation of his name and reputation from all the earth (vss. 18-21). Moreover, every word of the description is painfully applicable to Job himself, frightened by "terrors," with his skin consumed by disease, being "brought to the king of terrors" (death), having seen his habitation ruined by brimstone, and his offspring and descendants destroyed.

Notice should be taken especially of the imagery in verses 5 and 6, coming from a nomadic age with campfires and tent lights. The first line of verse 12 is a dramatic expression in English, but it might be better translated "His calamity is hungry," that is, it pursues him relentlessly. As the margin indicates, the first line of verse 13 needs an antecedent for "it," supposedly "disease." The imagery of the dried-up tree in verse 16 recalls Job's pathetic words in 14:7-12. Job had wondered if, like a tree coming to life, man might live again. Bildad warns that there is no such hope for him, for it is also true that the root of a tree finally dries up in the ground, and this is the prospect of the wicked.

Job Speaks (19:1-29)

To read chapter 19 of Job is clearly to come to a kind of climax. Although commentators on the book differ quite widely among themselves concerning the nature of the climax and on practically all the details of the chapter, there is almost entire agreement that the thought rises to a great height here.

You Torment Rather than Comfort Me (19:1-6)

The critical nature of this speech by Job is indicated by the abrupt way it begins. Without any preliminaries he charges the friends with incredible cruelty toward him. "How long," he asks —in imitation of Bildad's querulous beginning (18:1; see also 8:1)—"will you torment me?" All the verbs in verses 2 and 3 are dramatic, suggesting the exercise of harsh force. "Ten times" (vs. 3) means "often." Verse 4, addressed to the friends, is not to be understood as a confession of specific sin. As Job plainly indicates, he raises the *possibility* of error as a hypothesis only (for a similar expression see 7:20). Even granting the truth of the friends' charge, it still would prove nothing. The last line of verse 4 seems to mean that even if he *had* sinned (which he does not admit), it still would affect only himself and be his own affair, not the business of his friends. The following verse charges the friends with meddling for personal reasons—a remarkable insight into the unconscious motivation for much "comfort"—as they actually reveal their own insecurity and lack of strength.

Although it does not appear in the English translation of verse 6, Job here refers to a prior question of Bildad in 8:3. There Bildad had asked, in effect, "Does God do wrong?" As Bildad knows, it is fundamental to faith to answer "No." But absolute depth of despair cries "Yes!" In his case, Job charges, God has done wrong. The extreme to which Job has come is not merely that God is the author of his suffering; he now faces what the implication of that fact must be when taken together with his conviction of innocence, and he draws the terrible conclusion. Obviously this view would be totally destructive of all faith if it were allowed to stand. Chapter 19 shows how it is not allowed to stand, but it is not on the basis of rational argument that it is contraverted; rather, it is on the basis of Job's own experience of the nature of God.

God Has Estranged Me from All Help (19:7-22)

Before that point is reached, however, Job must go a great deal further in exploration of the awful consequences of the apparent hostility on the part of God. The reader ought not to minimize the character of Job's dilemma here as he recounts the effects of his tragedy on him personally (vss. 7-12) and its results in his total alienation from God and, indeed, from all humanity (vss. 13-19). Here is a classic statement of the total isolation to which an individual may be brought. It is also the darkness within which true light may begin to appear.

In his distress Job charges God with direct maliciousness, for Job's just cry of "Violence!" goes unanswered (vs. 7) and all way of escape is cut off by the tormentor (vs. 8). In verse 9 there is a reference to the happy prosperity which Job had once enjoyed but which is now gone, or it could be a reference to a corresponding state of spiritual exaltation from which Job is now degraded.

In verse 10 there is a clear allusion to Bildad's warning that hope does not apply in his case (18:16), a warning which was evoked by Job's previous reference to the "hope for a tree" (14:7). Here even that faint hope seems to be removed violently by God. The section ends with a dark picture of God as a relentless adversary preparing war against Job, a picture which recalls earlier imagery (see, for example, 16:14).

To this catalogue of hopeless effects Job now adds a recital of his complete alienation from all human means of help. The background for his thinking is furnished by his longing for someone who would take the part of an advocate or witness and who would carry on his case when he is dead. Hence he calls for one after the other of the possible witnesses, only to find them all not only indifferent but hostile. God's antagonism is painfully mirrored in human relationships, so that one of the most tragic elements of Job's situation is this estrangement of all men from him.

The "brethren" of verse 13 are, as the parallel to "acquaintances" shows, those who are related to him in the bond of the Covenant nation. In verses 14-16 he moves closer home, to kinsfolk, friends, and guests in his own circle, and to those who formerly had been his servants.

In verse 17 he obviously refers to members of his own family —wife and (literally) "the sons of my womb." The latter expression might be interpreted as Job's own children, although such a complete contradiction to the Prologue is hardly likely. It more probably means, as in the Revised Standard Version, the children of his own mother, that is, his literal brothers. These would be especially useful as witnesses were he not "loathsome" to them.

In view of the fact that the roll call of possible witnesses seems to be arranged in climactic order, rising to the culminating appeal to the friends, it is strange that verse 18 refers to "young children." These are children who mock Job ("talk against") as he tries to get up. It may be that these are children of the brethren of verse 17. At any rate, the last names on the list are those of his "intimate friends" themselves: Eliphaz, Bildad, and Zophar, whom Job has loved and whose heartless turning against him is his final crushing blow. His alienation is thus complete, a fact that he vividly states in verse 20, although the exact sense of the imagery is by no means clear. The first line must refer to his physical condition and probably implies extreme emaciation (clearly the meaning of the bones' cleaving to the "skin," but not so clearly of the bones' cleaving to the "flesh"). The second line is more difficult. The words have become a proverbial expression for a narrow escape of any kind, and such is apparently the meaning here. But it is impossible to say with certainty what "the skin of my teeth" means. Neither "gums" nor "lips" is entirely satisfactory, and none of the many changes suggested by commentators is much better. The most we can safely say is that Job by this expression means that he is left with virtually nothing. So it is that he comes in a final pathetic cry to his friends for pity, or for some token of sympathy, or even for simple recognition of his state—that he is forsaken by God and man.

Here is the book's sharpest picture of total alienation and aloneness. It is the kind of tragedy which even the Greek literary tragedies cannot match, for they lack the brighter background of former godliness against which to picture this blackness. For a parallel we must turn to the New Testament and to the one Righteous Sufferer who experienced forsakenness, of whose experience in Gethsemane and on the cross Job's tragedy is a faint foregleam. The differences are, of course, more marked than the similarities, especially in the fact that whereas Job is alienated *from* mankind, Jesus is forsaken by men but his very forsakenness is *for* mankind. Moreover, because our Lord thus endured the depths of the human condition, no one has again to stand entirely alone.

But God Himself Is My Help (19:23-29)

In these seven verses which bring Job's second speech to an end it is plain that (1) we have an important part of the discussion, (2) some climax of faith or religious experience is reached, and (3) we cannot be certain of the exact rendering of many expressions (see the differences between the Revised Standard Version and the older translations and the variations within the Revised Standard Version itself as indicated by the margin).

Verses 23 and 24 are the clearest of the seven and plainly show Job's longing for some kind of permanent record of his experience and of his defense. His "words" may be either the ones he has already spoken or the ones he will now speak, more probably the former. He pleads for a record that will outlast him, from which succeeding generations may read the justification of his innocence—that innocence which he is so far unable to establish. For a similar idea see 16:18, where he appeals to the "earth" to witness to his cause. In verse 23 he imagines that his defense could be "written" or "inscribed" (literally, "engraved") in a book or possibly a metal scroll (as, for example, the copper scrolls found recently at Qumran). In the following verse he longs for an even more enduring testimony, an inscription cut into rock by a tool of iron and lead. Thus his cry of "Innocent!" would stand through the centuries.

No such possibility is real. Consequently, bereft of all chance of defense or vindication in himself (19:1-12), in his fellow human beings (19:13-22), or in an objective record (19:23-24), he turns once again to God. We must remember that it is still the same God who, to Job, is the Author of his difficulties, the same God from whom he must necessarily feel himself estranged. This makes all the more remarkable Job's affirmation, as in a mighty statement of conviction he declares that God himself is his "Redeemer" or "Vindicator" (margin). The word is the one that is used in the Old Testament for the near kinsman who undertakes responsibility for a relative who has been wronged, one who acts on behalf of another. It is used also of God's redemptive activity on behalf of Israel. In his frantic roll call of acquaintances and relatives (vss. 13-22) Job has made a last desperate effort to find a "Vindicator" within the natural circle of human relationships; when that has failed he is thrown back on God. God himself is his security. Whatever future there is, is dependent on God. When Job has reached this state he has made a great advance, for he has literally been forced to the faith that God is the only One who can ultimately "justify" man. (That he is speaking of God seems to be clear from the application of the term "lives" and from the assertion of the following verse: "I shall see God.")

In the second line of verse 25 there is the indication that God who is Vindicator as well as Adversary (may we say *more* Vindicator than Adversary?) will witness for Job at the last. The reference to "dust" (margin) is obscure. It is hardly a term for "the earth"; nor can it be the dust of Job's destroyed body. Similarly it is difficult to see why a reference to the dust of original creation would be inserted here.

In verse 26 the Hebrew is extremely difficult to translate. It is not certain whether Job means he will see God from within his flesh or from without it. The former is more probable; it points, then, not to a vision of God before death but to a meeting with God beyond death, a meeting which would not be for Job a disembodied, "spiritual" experience (hence not in Sheol) but a real, fully personal encounter (see I Cor. 15:35-57).

Verse 27 confirms the fact that Job expects this meeting with the Vindicator God to be his own, and not that of someone else *for* him. It is to be his own joy and not that of a stranger. The phrases are repetitious, emphasizing strongly the personal quality of the statements.

If we are to take the translation of the last line of verse 27 (the original is very difficult) as in the Revised Standard Version, it must be understood as a reference to Job's physical and emotional exhaustion after the spiritual climax he has just reached. Verses 28 and 29 are obviously a parting warning to the friends that, in the light of his present conviction, he knows that terrible judgment awaits them for their pursuit of him with false assumptions about his guilt.

Such an interpretation of this section is not without difficulties, and it leaves unexplained some of the obscurities of the passage. But in spite of these, and in spite of the difficult state of the Hebrew text here, we must not miss the fact that a great insight is set forth in these verses. It comes, as is often the case in the Book of Job, precisely when a depth of despair is plumbed. Moreover, this height is not maintained hereafter in unwavering and continuous faith. But this makes it more real and more directed toward us. When earthly security is completely removed, and when there is no future at all, then God becomes our true Security and pledges himself for the future. In this sense there is great justification in seeing this as an anticipation of the New Testament good news.

Zophar Speaks (20:1-29)

The Joy of the Godless Is Temporary (20:1-11)

Zophar begins with an abrupt explanation. His opening "therefore" may indicate that heretofore he has been restraining himself and now must justify the fact that he speaks. It is apparent that he has been somewhat troubled, not just by Job's general attitude, but especially by the conviction Job has just voiced and the solemn warning he has given the friends. It is even possible that Zophar is represented as having temporarily wavered in his dogmatism but as having crushed down any unsettling thoughts and returned to the safety of the absolute principle set out in verses 4 and 5.

Verses 6 and 7 indicate that Zophar is willing to accept the fact of a *temporary* prosperity for the godless; but he is certain that it is only temporary, and later he will assert that it is not satisfying. The wicked man "will perish." Job has remarked on the apparent hopelessness of man's prospect: "Man dies . . . and where

is he?" (14:10). Zophar says that the question must be asked not
of man in general but only of the wicked man, whose life is like
a "dream" or a "vision of the night" (vs. 8; for the use of similar
imagery for life in general see Ps. 90:4-5). In verse 10 Zophar
moves on to the thought that the prosperity of the wicked passes
away with him; his children are reduced to beggary or will have
to pay back the gain he had gotten unjustly (understanding
"their hands" for "his hands" in verse 10). Verse 11 sums up in
the basic contention that whatever strength the godless may seem
to have will perish with him and come to nothing.

Prosperity Is Bitter to the Wicked (20:12-19)

At verse 12 the thought shifts to the bitterness of such prosperity as does come to the wicked. It brings no real enjoyment;
what seems to be sweet turns bitter (vss. 12-14); riches are not
retained but become a poison to the one who takes them (vss.
15-16). The result is that the ungodly man has no lasting profit
from his evil (vss. 17-18; the figure of "honey and curds" is a familiar one for peaceful prosperity). In verse 19 Zophar again
comes to a summary, this time in a statement that is prophetic in
tone. Here he might be an Amos or an Isaiah, speaking the moral
truth that prosperity founded on injustice does not last in God's
world.

The Life of Evil Men Is Terrible (20:20-29)

In the closing part of his speech Zophar turns to the terrible
nature of the life which the wicked man is doomed to live. His
life is not only short and his prosperity bitter; his whole existence
is marked by ceaseless terror. Here Zophar goes beyond the
limits of even general truth as he describes the wicked man as
never knowing a moment free from misery. The characteristics of
this misery are counted off: unenduring prosperity (vs. 22), God's
unremitting anger (vs. 23), no hope of escape (vs. 24), terror of
death (vs. 25), darkness and fire (vs. 26), and a flood of destruction (vs. 28). All this, Zophar declares, is "the wicked man's
portion from God," and it is so because heaven itself will be his
accuser and earth his destroyer (vs. 27). Again it is evident that
Zophar has learned well the word of the prophets. Unfortunately
he is one of the too large group in all ages who have made the
truth of the past an inviolable barrier against new understanding
and insight into the present.

Job Speaks (21:1-34)

As at the close of the first round of discussion (chs. 12-14), so here, the author represents Job as finally coming to deal with the main point of the friends' speeches. They have drawn in great detail the picture of the wicked man living in terror and despair, facing imminent destruction, afflicted all his days, and never really enjoying his prosperity. This picture Job now systematically destroys. He attacks it from every side and in the end leaves no line of it unchallenged. In so doing he comes close to affirming the exact opposite of the friends' contention, and to declaring that the wicked man alone is truly prosperous, happy, and secure.

My Conclusions Are the Opposite of Yours (21:1-6)

In harmony with the usual practice Job begins with a justification for his words. Everything he says points to the radical nature of the stand he is to take. He warns the friends to be prepared for an appalling revelation which will put great strain on them (vs. 5). Even he is "dismayed" at the prospect (vs. 6). However, he justifies the extremity of his language and his position by the fact that his quarrel is not the usual complaint against man but is an extraordinary one against God (vs. 4). All this means that the friends should give the more careful consideration to what he will now say, as he asks that silence be substituted for their previous "consolation" (vs. 2). At any rate he is determined to speak, even though he anticipates nothing but mockery in return (vs. 3; "mock on" is singular, indicating that it is addressed to Zophar).

As I See It, the Wicked Are Happy (21:7-16)

Job sees quite a different picture from the one Zophar has so vividly traced. Moreover, he regards his own view as obvious, for without preliminary statement he abruptly asks why it is that the wicked live to ripe age and prosper all of their lives (vs. 7). In contrast to Zophar's description of the transient security of the wicked, of his loneliness, of his terror and misery, Job speaks of the wicked as enjoying full and uninterrupted security, surrounded by happy, playing children. Such men are immune from the judgments of God (vs. 9) and even have a kind of automatic insurance against accidental loss (vs. 10).

Verse 13 is a summary of Job's view; the life of the wicked is described as one of unbroken prosperity and his death as unmarked by long illness or suffering. In verses 14 and 15 Job makes it plain that he is speaking of the actively wicked. These are not the merely indifferent or careless, but are the ones who have reasoned things out and who have therefore deliberately rejected the way of righteousness and turned from the service of God as from a profitless endeavor. The three friends have insisted that prosperity is the reward which God gives to the righteous. On the contrary, says Job, the unrighteous man knows that prosperity comes only from his own evil endeavor and that righteousness gains no reward. To such men their prosperity is "in their [own] hand" rather than from God, and so they live and plan without thought of the Almighty (vs. 16, the last line of which may be translated, as in the ancient Greek version, "the counsel of the wicked is far from *him*.")

The Life and Destiny of the Wicked Are Peaceful (21:17-34)

Job demolishes one after another of the friends' superficial judgments about the life of unrighteous men. Bildad has said that "the light of the wicked is put out" (18:5-6), and that "calamity is ready for his stumbling" (18:12); Zophar has said that "God will send his fierce anger into him" (20:23). Job challenges each of these conclusions and declares that such is by no means the case (21:17). A fundamental assumption of the orthodox view was that the wicked are "like chaff which the wind drives away" (Ps. 1:4). Job declares that this simply is not true in his experience or not true enough to serve as a rule of life.

In verses 19-21 Job proceeds to cut the ground from any attempt to support the popular view by an appeal to succeeding generations. Exodus 20:5 had declared that God visits "the iniquity of the fathers upon the children to the third and the fourth generation," meaning that the effects and punishment of sin were long-lived and continued beyond the life of the sinner. This was taken, however, to mean that God at times *postponed* judgment, allowing the sinner to escape but visiting later generations with wrath. Such a view Job indignantly rejects as unrealistic and unfair. The wicked man, he declares, ought to be punished himself, for he would have no real concern for his descendants, provided he escaped in his own lifetime (see also 14:21-22).

Verse 22 is a break in Job's otherwise steady argument. It may be that he is exclaiming over the inscrutable nature of God's judgments, utterly beyond human comprehension. On the other hand, he may be longing for an opportunity to "teach God" and at least reconstruct life more nearly according to his own desires.

In verses 23-26 Job continues his theme, restating his conviction that God's operations in the world are indiscriminate (see also 9:22-24). Death comes to good and bad alike, the only difference is that the wicked man has had an easy, secure, and prosperous life, and the good man has had not so much as a taste of prosperity. There is no difference in their deaths.

The thought leads Job to a final culminating illustration of his view. There *is*, in fact, a difference in the death of the wicked and the death of the righteous: the wicked man even has a fine funeral! The friends have spoken of the ephemeral nature of the evil man's home and security (for example, 8:15-18; 15:34; 18:15; 20:26-27), asking in effect, "Where is the tent in which the wicked dwelt?" Job declares contemptuously that it is everywhere. They should ask people who get around, who will tell them that the facts of life point to the safety of the wicked in the day of calamity and to his immunity from all retributive justice. Particularly they will testify to the final evidence of this immunity as they describe the way the wicked man's body is borne to its tomb, honored and respected, and accompanied by crowds of mourners. Job adds, in bitter irony, that even the clods of earth thrown on his grave are "sweet to him." This is the way life is, and the words of the friends are "empty nothings" and "falsehood."

When Job's position is contrasted with the position of the friends, as stated for example by Zophar in chapter 20, it is easy to see that both are unrealistic extremes. Both, moreover, betray a fundamental error: that life itself furnishes incontrovertible and conclusive evidence about the workings of God. Only when life is free from bondage to sin and free from the disfiguring mark of sin—as in the Incarnate Life—can it bear unambiguous witness to God.

THE THIRD ROUND OF DISCUSSION

Job 22:1—31:40

Eliphaz Speaks (22:1-30)

God Judges You for Your Wickedness (22:1-11)

Eliphaz is consistent in his view of God as transcendent, that is, as far above the life and affairs of men. At times his theology pushes him to the extremes of deism, with a God who is not only transcendent but actually absentee (see comment on 4:18-19). This seems to be the case here, for in verses 2 and 3 he declares that man's righteousness and wisdom, whether absolute or relative, are of no concern whatsoever to God. Such an exaggerated view is of course completely at odds with the entire Old Testament revelation which, although viewing God as omnipotent and truly holy, nevertheless knows him to be concerned with the whole life of the world, individual, family, and nation.

In verses 4-11 Eliphaz leaves undeveloped this first theme and turns briskly to a personal attack on Job. In line with the fundamental presuppositions of the friends, namely that suffering was retribution for sin, and with his inability to explain Job's suffering as either only apparent or ephemeral, he begins to list the actual situations of sin which might have caused the tragedy. For the first time Job is charged with specific sins, although the friends have hinted before at his sinful nature. Here Eliphaz strikes in the dark, and certainly there is no evidence for any of his charges. (Job refutes most of them in chapter 31.) Eliphaz guesses that Job has been unjust to the needy (vs. 6), that he has omitted the acts of kindness required by the Law (vs. 7), that he has supported the rich and the powerful in their grasping (vs. 8), or that he has denied the rightful pleas of the ones who have been dispossessed (vs. 9). Something of this sort, Eliphaz is saying, is the explanation of Job's present life of terror and darkness (vss. 10-11). It is interesting to note that when the list of sins is thus drawn up it concentrates on ethical and social misdeeds, a remarkable sign of the effectiveness of the prophetic teaching.

Perhaps You Think God Does Not Know (22:12-20)

Eliphaz next returns to his major emphasis, the transcendence of God. He hazards the thought that Job, believing also in a God far removed (vs. 12), has imagined that he was safe to speak error and blasphemy. In verses 13-14 Eliphaz seems to be referring to Job's words, either in a deliberate misquotation or deliberate misinterpretation. The nearest parallel in Job's speech is 21:22, which clearly does not mean what Eliphaz intimates. After repeating his basic contention that wicked men have no security, Eliphaz again quotes Job (vs. 17, see 21:14a, 15a; vs. 18, see 21:16). This time the quotation is more accurate, although a different application is made. In Job's speech it is a matter of the prosperity which the wicked enjoy in spite of their disregard of God; Eliphaz uses the words to point up the destruction that comes to the wicked, to the delight of the righteous, who have been mistreated by them (vss. 19-20).

Your Only Hope Is Repentance (22:21-30)

Although Eliphaz' speech is generally hostile in tone, it does end with an appeal to Job rather than with blanket condemnation. He counsels Job to "return to the Almighty." This time he means not merely a patient waiting for God, but actual repentance. Since he is convinced that some definite sin lay at the root of Job's misfortune, his best advice is that Job "humble" himself and "remove unrighteousness." With what must be taken as complete indifference to the actual situation, he further advises Job to give up his confidence in gold and other material treasures, and to make God his only treasure and delight (vss. 24-25). Once the speaker has embarked on this stream of argument he moves swiftly and smoothly to the imagined happy issue. All of this has been said before; its repetition is a reminder of the bankruptcy of the friends and of their total indifference to the facts. Eliphaz' parting promise—and these are the last words we hear from him —is pathetic: "He delivers the innocent man; you will be delivered . . ." He has no other solution to offer, although this one is mockery. It stands at odds with the whole biblical message, for deliverance is never on the grounds of man's innocency or the cleanness of his hands but always on the basis of the grace of God.

Job Speaks (23:1—24:25)

The chapter, like many that follow it to the end of the book, poses difficulties for translators. The Hebrew text here is often uncertain and recourse must be had to ancient translations and to conjecture, as the multiplicity of marginal notes in the Revised Standard Version attests. In this commentary not all the possible renderings will be discussed, nor will every place where there is uncertainty be noted. These can usually be determined from the margin, and where there is no comment it is to be assumed that the translation of the Revised Standard Version represents as good a solution as any proposed.

I Cannot Find God (23:1-17)

In the first half of his speech Job complains that it is impossible to come into the presence of God with any sort of accusation directed at his governance of the world. It is quite in the mood of Job here to remark that, like the nation, God cannot be sued. The image of the courtroom, which has been implicit all along, now dominates the entire discussion. Job has a case against God, or at least against God's supposedly righteous rule, but he has no way of making this case so that it will be heard and credited.

He recognizes that it is, at root, a complaint against God. In verse 1 he declares that his "complaint" (a legal term) is "rebellious" (see the margin). He does not deny that it sets him in the unenviable position of rebel against God. And it is significant that in the last speeches by Job this feeling of rebelliousness heightens. It is true that he has, by and large, settled in his mind the *personal* outcome of his tragedy (see ch. 19). But the larger question of God's righteous control of human affairs is another matter, and here Job is by no means content. He will not be stayed from his purpose; he cannot even restrain himself. (Verse 2b is probably, "My hand is heavy on my groaning," meaning that he has tried, in vain, to hold back the rebellious words.)

These words are not restrained, and they break forth like a torrent in a great statement of man's inability to bring the Almighty to account. Wherever he goes, and however he tries, Job is unable to bring God into the courtroom where judgment might be rendered by normal human standards. In such a courtroom the human complainant might learn the nature of the indictment against him, and even though the divine Judge (or Defendant) would be incomparably the more powerful, at least the case could be heard (vss. 5-6). Job's confidence in his blamelessness and in the rightness of his position appears in verse 7, as he indicates that he cannot yet think in terms of any other relationship to God than that of rectitude of life. Here he unconsciously echoes the thought of Eliphaz (22:30).

Verses 8 and 9 expand the impossibility of subpoenaing God for a legal proceeding. The terms "forward," "backward," "on the left hand," and "to the right hand" are equivalent to the points of the compass. Job thus declares that although God may be present and active to the widest bounds of human life (vs. 9, see margin) he is unapproachable and remains so completely hidden that man can have no real dealing with him.

The confidence in himself which Job feels throughout appears again in verse 10. If instead of "but" we understand "for" here, the verse is an ironic explanation of God's hiddenness. He hides precisely because he knows he is in the wrong in Job's case.

Eliphaz has counseled Job to "receive instruction" from God, and to "lay up his words" in his heart (22:22). Job declares that he has in fact done this but that it is of no effect (23:12-17). He faces the certainty of divine action without divine revelation, and is overcome by the prospect. It is absolute mystery; it points up the meaninglessness of all existence, and before it he can only fear (vss. 13-16). The last verse of the chapter is difficult. As the Revised Standard Version has it, the words are an amplification of the mysteriousness and the meaninglessness to which Job has just referred. Another possibility, keeping the negative (as in the margin), is that Job recalls Eliphaz' words in 22:11 where he says that Job's "light is darkened" so that he cannot see. Job may be saying here that it is not because of darkness that he is "hemmed in," or because of a shadow before his face, but because of God's arbitrary and senseless activity. He is overwhelmed, not by inability to see, but by too clear a sight of what must seem to be total indifference in God.

God Pays No Attention (24:1-17; 18-25?)

In the interpretation suggested above, 23:17 prepares the way for the outburst of chapter 24, which turns from the horror of a God who remains completely hidden to the multiplied horror of a God who is apathetic to all moral distinctions and indifferent to all injustices in life. In a speech of deeply tragic dimensions Job pictures the fate of those who have gotten the short end of life, the "have nots," his description betraying the deep solicitude and concern he feels over such distresses.

The section opens with a difficult verse. The Revised Standard Version represents it as a protest by Job against the fact that God is immune to judgment. The "times" and "days" would refer to seasons of judgment, such as a court session, when accumulated wrongs could be righted or at least given a satisfactory explanation.

The speaker then (vss. 2-12) gives a list of the kinds of injustice which might well be dealt with in such a court session. Most prominent among them is the injustice done to those whose inheritance has been appropriated, the poor who are driven out into the wilderness, who must suffer physical hardship, and whose difficult labor increases the wealth of the wicked. Verse 9 is a parenthetical expression amplifying the thought of verses 2-4. The whole description reaches a powerful climax in verse 12, which sums up the desperation of the poor and the wounded and at the same time stresses the indifference of God.

This illustration of rampant injustice is now paralleled by others: a whole group of rebels against the light, who love darkness as a cover for their misdeeds—murderers, adulterers, thieves (vss. 14-16). These denizens of the night constitute for Job one more sickening evidence that no moral principle operates in the world, a conclusion he has voiced before (ch. 9) but never expanded as here. The impression grows that, as a careful lawyer, he is accumulating evidence in the case he would present, although as yet he lacks courtroom and judge.

At verse 18 it is evident that a strong break comes in the thought. Verses 18-20 can hardly be the words of Job, at least not in such close connection with what he has just said. The Revised Standard Version recognizes the difficulty and interprets these verses as a quotation by Job of the position of the friends (adding the words "You say" for which there is no equivalent in the original text). It is certainly true that sections like 8:18; 15:30-31; 18:16-20; and 20:4-29 represent the friends as holding the position set forth here, although these exact words do not appear in their speeches. If this interpretation be adopted, then Job quotes the ideas of the friends for the purpose of refuting them, and verses 21-25 form his rebuttal. Thus he seems to declare that the security of the wicked is not at all ephemeral, but quite solid, and that it is itself the gift of God (vss. 22-23). Verse 24, then, would be not a picture of the uncertainty of the life of the wicked but the opposite: the fact is that they are exalted ("a little while" means only in common with all human life), but, unlike the rest of humanity, the wicked slip away quietly, with a peaceful death. They do not die prematurely (as Job) but are cut off like a full head of grain, that is, after they have come to maturity. This, Job says, can be disputed by no one, and the context implies that this "no one" includes God.

Some interpreters offer an alternate solution which seems simpler and more in harmony with the thought of the book. This is that verses 18-24, in part or as a whole, are the words of one of the friends, either Bildad or, more probably, Zophar. They are misplaced here, perhaps by intent. It is possible that some timid editor, feeling that Job's words have gone too far in the direction of blasphemy, consequently modified them by inserting this opposite view, using words which in the original form of the book belonged to one of the friends. In so doing he attributed to Job a view which actually negates what Job has just said, and to which Job would never subscribe (see comment on ch. 27). If this is true, then "You say" in verse 18 should be omitted from the English translation. Verses 22 and 23, moreover, would then be understood as an admission that while God *seems* to give security to the wicked, it is in reality only ephemeral and before long the wicked are carried off like a dry weed or like the head of grain cut from the stalk.

Bildad Speaks (25:1-6)

A glance at the text is sufficient indication that the structure of the book is out of joint here. Bildad's third speech is so short that some explanation must be offered. The possibilities can be reduced to two. The first is that the author by shortening the speeches of the friends, even by altogether omitting a third speech by Zophar, wished to symbolize the defeat of the friends in the debate. If this is the case it is a rather subtle device, and if such was the author's intent it could easily have failed in its purpose.

The second possibility has to do with possible dislocation of the original order of the book. When we try to assign reasons for such disorder we find no absolutely secure ground. It is conceivable that actual physical disrepair of manuscripts led to faulty rearrangement. It is also conceivable that some parts of speeches were deliberately moved in order to achieve what would seem to be a more orthodox effect.

God Alone Is Great (25:1-6)

These verses form a kind of doxology, reciting the majesty and power of God in such a way as to emphasize the littleness of man. This is, of course, in no sense an answer to Job's preceding speech; rather, it intensifies the problem with which he deals there. Verses 2 and 3 stress God's absolute and unyielding control, and dwell on the effect of his control in heaven where his absolute dominion produces universal "fear." The phrase "he makes peace" refers to God's power to quell rebellion (a reference to Job's complaint?) but also conveys the idea of God's power to establish a condition of peace. The line is like the second line of verse 3, which in a striking way stresses the total rule of God but does so in an image ("light") which carries the idea of blessing.

These ideas are not, however, expanded by Bildad. Rather he draws the conclusion that God's greatness and his universal dominion serve to illuminate the uncleanness of man.

Job Speaks (26:1-14?)

Such Words Give No Help (26:1-4)

Verses 1-4 are clearly a rebuke of the friends, for their words of advice, which were meant to be helpful, were not so at all. Some interpreters see in these verses a continuation of the speech of Bildad (omitting verse 1), and regard them as that speaker's reminder to Job of the way in which formerly he has been quick to offer the orthodox formulae of advice, and of the fact that the views he has just uttered must represent some other "spirit." Others see that the connection with 25:1-6 is not at all clear and prefer to regard 26:2-4 as the *opening* of Bildad's third speech, assigning 25:1-6 to the third speech of Zophar.

Still others, with perhaps better reason, agree with the heading of 26:1 and see these verses as a part of Job's reply to Bildad. If this is the case then the words are scornful and sarcastic throughout. Their nearest parallels are 6:25-26 and 16:2-5, but here Job's bitterness is even more pronounced, and he even implies that

Bildad's speech is not his own view but that he parrots another, or repeats what an evil spirit taught him.

God Is Incomprehensible in Power (26:5-14)

If these verses (5-14) are read immediately after 25:1-6, it will be apparent how naturally they fit the thought of Bildad's last speech. For this reason, and because they represent a point of view which is not in harmony with Job's main contention as the book nears its climax, they are usually assigned to Bildad. The verses are an extended recital of God's limitless and essentially incomprehensible power, and as such could, of course, have been spoken by any of the participants.

In connection with Bildad's other words it can be seen that the power of God is represented as operating first in heaven (25:1-6) and then in Sheol (26:5-6). "The shades" are the inhabitants of Sheol; "the waters" is a reference to "the water under the earth" (Exod. 20:4), the abyss upon which the earth was thought to have been founded. "Abaddon" is a synonym for Sheol (see 28:22; 31:12; Prov. 15:11), meaning literally "destruction" (so also in the New Testament the similar Greek word "Apollyon" refers to the Destroyer, see Rev. 9:11).

The image which appears in the following verses is that of God's creative power by which he defeated and brought under control the powers of chaos, symbolized in the darkness and the waters, and by which he continually sustains the earth, hanging it "upon nothing." In verse 7 the reference to "the void" recalls the Genesis account of creation (Gen. 1:2), as do the following verses with reference to the binding of the waters. The word "moon" in verse 9 is a guess; other possibilities are "throne" or, better, "tent," referring to God's dwelling. The "circle" in verse 10 describes the limiting boundary which God has fixed, so that the waters of chaos and the darkness will not again overwhelm the earth (see also Prov. 8:27; Job 38:8, 11). In verse 11 there may be a reference to the upheaval consequent upon God's creative act, or it may be a reference to an earthquake which, although severe, does not destroy the earth itself. "Rahab" in verse 12 is a common name for the primitive chaotic power, usually symbolized as a dragon, defeated by God in creation (see comment on 3:8; 7:12; 9:13), also depicted in verse 13. There can be no doubt that the poet used an ancient mythological picture, neither can there be any doubt that he did not accept it as fact.

It is imagery, powerful and informing, but it is not the truth itself. The truth which appears strongly in this doxology is that God is in full control of his creation. Creation and man's existence are continuously maintained by God and only by him. If it were not for the exercise of his power, the forces of evil, of chaos, the darkness, and the waters of the abyss, would sweep over and destroy.

With such a profound truth before the speaker it is noticeable that the conclusion he draws is not the conclusion of faith but of an obtuse kind of agnosticism. All of the evidences of God's power, even the supreme evidence of the act of creation, are but the fringes of the power itself. Therefore man can only resign himself to a fractional understanding.

Job Speaks (27:1-23?)

Although in the present form of the Book of Job chapters 27-31 are represented as belonging to the final speech of Job, it is evident from the content itself that there are some difficulties associated with this view. First, there is the fact, already mentioned, that Zophar is not given a third and final speech. Second, 27:7-23 forms a unit which sounds strikingly like the position of the three friends and which is in part difficult to assign to Job. Third, chapter 28 is another unit, self-contained and complete in itself, a poem dealing with the impossibility of finding "Wisdom," again an idea somewhat out of context. Finally, there are two introductory statements in this entire section, one at 27:1 and the other at 29:1, both of which are unlike the common introduction "then Job answered" (see, for example, 16:1 and 19:1; see also 20:1).

Taken all together these difficulties point once more to some sort of dislocation of the original order of the book. Each one can be dealt with and resolved separately; but as a whole the problem is not easily solved.

Still I Will Not Recant (27:1-6)

This is clearly Job; the words could have been spoken by no other. And this is Job at his most confident stand. Here he is Prometheus, holding on to his right, not hurling defiance at God but steadfastly maintaining the justice of his cause. The insistent challenges of the friends have now in the end served only to clarify and crystallize his own thoughts. There is a noticeable change from his former uncertainties. Where before he has betrayed elements of indecision and uncertainty, here there is only calm assurance, an absolute certainty.

The strength and confidence he feels are evident in the opening words which form the introductory formula to an oath. "As the Lord lives" is the common formula, although the form "As God lives" appears also (see II Sam. 2:27). Job swears by the very God to whom his complaint is addressed and who is himself the subject of that complaint. As long as Job lives (vs. 3), which will not be long, two things will remain unchanged: he will not lie and he will not deny the fundamental fact of his "integrity" (see chs. 1 and 2). In verse 6 he makes the strong statement that not only is his righteousness unblemished (see 9:21), but his conscience is also untroubled. Elihu later refers to this remarkable confidence of Job (compare 34:5 with 27:6 and 2). And the Greek translation of the last line of verse 6 appears also in Paul's words in I Corinthians 4:4. However, a good deal of the difference between the Book of Job and the New Testament is to be seen in the contrast between these two passages. Where Job can say, "My heart does not reproach me," Paul declares, "I am not aware of anything against myself," and then adds out of his Christian faith, "but I am not thereby acquitted."

The Godless Have No Hope (27:7-23?)

Verses 7-10 clearly form a denial of any hope to the "godless." God will not give hope when such a man has been cut off, God will not hear his prayer even if he calls, and the unrighteous man himself finds none of the delightful solaces of faith.

Is this Job? If so, then he is strongly reiterating his own righteousness (see vs. 6) and reassuring himself that as poor as its rewards are, for him they are still better than the hopelessness of the wicked. Moreover, he may be affirming that although the wicked have, as he has constantly affirmed, the best in life and death, they have no hope for life or vindication after death, a hope which he has reached (ch. 19) and which is his own personal resolution of his burning agony.

In this sense the words can be assigned to Job. And yet it is easy to see that they do not exactly sound like him and at best represent some modification of his former position. Consequently many interpreters see in these words another misplaced portion of one of the final speeches of the friends, possibly Zophar. The problem remains, however, for the thought is difficult to connect with anything the friends have said, and it is not clear why either of them should refer to his "enemy." No final solution can be reached.

This is also true of verses 11-12, which again appear to be Job's words. They seem to be addressed to the friends and to anticipate some new or strong statement on the part of Job, a statement of what the friends have "seen" but apparently not understood. But what is this revelation? Is it the position set forth in verses 13-23? If so, it must be said that this is precisely the position of the friends, so much so that its phrasing as well as its thought can be paralleled in their other speeches. Some interpreters prefer to make these words introductory to chapter 28, where the connection is better.

To come to verses 13-23 is to reach the basic problem. Here, it is abundantly clear, is a strong, unrelieved statement of the unhappy fate of the wicked, his "portion" and his inheritance. And it turns out to be exactly what the friends have maintained all along! If the wicked man has children, they perish or starve (vss. 14-15; compare 5:4; 18:15, 17, 19); his possessions vanish (vss. 16-19; compare 15:29, 33; 20:18-19, 20-22, 26, 28); he is the subject of unremitting terror (vss. 20-23; compare 15:20-24; 18: 11-14; 20:23-27). The images are sharp and mainly clear. In verse 18 the Revised Standard Version's "like a spider's web" is a guess and incorporates an image which is used frequently in the Wisdom Literature (see Job 8:14-15); but the Hebrew "like the moth" is not impossible to understand and is paralleled in Job 4: 19. Verse 22 makes "the east wind" the subject of the verb, although the margin is possible, paralleling 20:23-25.

Again the question must be asked: Is this Job? Or is it a misplaced fragment of a lost speech of Zophar? In favor of the latter it must be agreed that the imagery and the thought are clearly harmonious with Zophar's manner and ideas. It is easy to see, moreover, that such a statement might have been assigned to Job by an overcautious editor who feared that the hero had gone too far in his denial that any moral principle operated in the world.

Can we say, on the other hand, that these words could have been Job's in the original work? In so doing we would have to say as well that the author meant thereby to modify Job's excesses. Such modification would seem to be so strong that it would virtually negate everything that has been said before.

One other line of reasoning is a possibility, namely, that Job here is represented as quoting the friends in a kind of deliberate parody. In favor of this it may be pointed out that once before he has clearly done this, if 24:18-20 is the speech of Job. If this is the case, then verbal similarities to previous speeches of the friends would be expected; however, this is a hypothesis and does not completely solve the difficulties, for the words themselves do not indicate that they are a quotation, and the connection with what precedes and what follows is not smooth. Once again we are left with a difficulty which is insoluble on the basis of the evidence we now have. But it must be affirmed that this difficulty in no way detracts from either an understanding of the Book of Job or a full appreciation of its content.

A Poem on Wisdom (28:1-28)

Chapter 28 in its entirety forms another unresolved problem so far as the unity of the last part of the Book of Job is concerned. As the book now stands it is a part of the final speech of Job, for no separate introductory formula is given to it. Like other parts of the same section, however, its content is not particularly like the rest of Job's views as expressed elsewhere, although here the difference is not so strongly marked.

The chapter may be a relatively independent poem on the impossibility of achieving "wisdom" by man's efforts, incorporated into the structure of the book by the author or an editor. It is probably intended to reflect the thought of Job rather than that of the friends and may fairly be understood as an expression of Job's feeling that the quest in which he has been engaged is virtually impossible of success (but see vs. 28).

It is clear that the first part of the poem is built on an extended image, the search for wisdom being contrasted with the search for precious metals. The poet has given elaborate treatment to the image, incorporating many easily recognizable details of mining operations in ancient times.

Man Is Able to Discover Precious Metals (28:1-11)

These verses describe the process whereby metals and precious stones were mined, for example in the copper and turquoise mines of the Sinai peninsula. The opening of the shafts, the descent of the miners on ropes, and even the displacement of earth and streams are all vividly described. Verse 5 remarks on the wonder that while the calm earth continues to bring forth its grain, underneath extensive and destructive forces work. The shafts are so far below the surface that even the keen-eyed bird and the proud king of beasts do not know of their existence. Thus man in his power is able to bring to light "the thing that is hid" (vs. 11).

But Wisdom Cannot Be Found (28:12-22)

Man may discover all that is hid—all save one thing, and that is wisdom. The irony of man's life, moreover, is that all of the precious fortunes he *can* discover cannot purchase the one thing that is needful. Man cannot attain to wisdom, either by search (vss. 12-14) or by purchase (vss. 15-19). Finally, the conclusion is reached that it is completely "hid" from the sight of man, so that his deepest shafts of insight cannot reach it, for even Destruction ("Abaddon") and "Death" cannot supply such a store.

God Has Wisdom (28:23-28)

Here the poet underlines the basic position of the whole wisdom movement: Wisdom belongs to God, not to man. God knows the location of wisdom and made use of it in the creation of the world; he uses it still in maintaining creation. Wisdom for man, then, can only be to reverence God and to obey him ("fear" in verse 28 is properly "reverence").

This conclusion is by no means inappropriate in the mouth of Job, nor, in fact, is the entire poem. It should be remembered that Job does not anywhere claim independent wisdom. It is not his desire to "know" in the metaphysical sense. He wants an *answer* from God. Here, then, near the end of the discussion he rehearses for himself the ancient principles of Hebrew wisdom, and reminds himself that wisdom is never the result of man's effort but only of God's offer or of God's speaking. Here the poet shows himself thoroughly in harmony with the mainstream of the wisdom movement, the poem paralleling in many respects the fundamental assumptions of the Book of Proverbs, or at least of its introductory position (see the parallel between Job 28:23-28 and Proverbs 8: 22-31 where "wisdom" speaks).

Although some difficulties remain in regarding the poem in chapter 28 as a part of the original book, perhaps there are fewer difficulties in this view than in any other. If it be the true one, then it is plain that in this concluding section of Job the author is giving a kind of summary statement of Job's best and truest positions. Basic to them all is this confidence, not unlike the rest of his speeches, although more violently expressed elsewhere—the confidence that ultimately wisdom can only be had on God's terms and as the gift of God. Both in language and in thought we are not very far from the great speeches of the Almighty which later close the book.

Job's Final Testimony (29:1—31:40)

In the present arrangement of the Book of Job, which must represent substantially the author's original intent, the orderly arrangement of the conversation between Job and his three friends is brought to a close with a summary speech by Job, framed in rather calm language, as Job makes his case. And in these chapters it is clear that it is precisely a legal case that he is making. From midway in the book Job is represented as in search of a courtroom and a court session in which man might present a legitimate case against the Almighty. At the same time the conviction has grown on him, and doubtless on the reader, that no such courtroom or session is available to man. God does not provide "times" when he may be arraigned, and he does not answer to man's subpoenas.

It is, therefore, all the more striking that in the end, with this disheartening truth in full view—as it is, for instance, in chapter 28—Job still makes his case and enters his complaint. These chapters are remarkably like the closing speech of a skilled lawyer, summing up the evidence, presenting the facts, reinforcing the legitimacy of the plea. That it is all done against the background of a seemingly empty courtroom gives greater nobility to the proceedings. Job's words echo in the emptiness. As far as he can tell there is no judge on the bench, no jury in the box, no audience in the room. And still he must make the case. He climbs, as it were, into the witness stand, and becomes complainant, lawyer, witness, jury, and judge, declaring, testifying to, and pronouncing on his own innocence.

The Evidence of the Past (29:1-25)

The basis of Job's complaint is the same that we find throughout the discussion; it is the fundamental fact, accepted in the Prologue, that he is "a blameless and upright man, who fears God and turns away from evil" (1:8). In chapter 29 that fact is elaborated and established in a passage of great beauty and power.

In reflection on his past Job draws the picture of a life that was prosperous and happy—but prosperous and happy because it was rooted in friendship with God and expressed itself in piety and justice. Job is not merely bewailing the departure of bygone days —he is rather agonizing once more over the loss of God's blessing and, therefore, of God.

His earlier life is described first of all as one in direct and confident relationship to God. Those were days when God "watched over" him (vs. 2), when the "lamp" of God was over him, a familiar symbol of God's presence and direction (vs. 3), when the "friendship" or perhaps better the "secret" of God was his (vs. 4), in fact, when the Almighty was himself with him (vs. 5a).

The commonly expected results of such a relationship are then reviewed. These include the presence of his children (vs. 5b), wealth (vs. 6), and general respect among the leaders of the people (vss. 7-10). The "gate" is of course the place where legal and community matters were settled, so that these verses give the picture of Job as a leader among leaders, one who is respected by all groups—young and old, princes and nobles. This is, again, elaboration of the suggestion in the Prologue that Job "was the greatest of all the people of the east" (1:3).

Verses 11-20 carry the thought still further in examining the character of the man who enjoyed such extraordinary blessings and respect. Here is the amplification of what is meant when Job is said to be "blameless and upright" (1:8). He was so regarded because of his actions, which gave evidence of his inner probity and rectitude. In this picture he stands as the ideal of Old Testament righteousness, a man of ethical dealings, with particular concern for those who had no strength in themselves. His concern and help went out to the poor, the fatherless, the widow, the blind, the lame, and the stranger. Against the unrighteous who preyed upon such unfortunates Job stood as their strong defender.

As such Job could naturally be confident of two things. One was his own righteousness, which became his glory and his pride (vs. 14). That, for all its greatness, it was measured against a narrow standard of human affairs does not yet appear to him. The second confidence was that he would reach a comfortable and ripe old age (vss. 18-20). (There is a possibility that the second line of verse 18 should read "and I shall multiply my days as the phoenix," a translation that would afford a better parallel to the first line.) In the place of both confidences he has now only despair and uncertainty.

As a closing and climactic detail in this picture of his former state of righteousness and blessedness, Job turns back to the respect in which he was once held (vss. 21-25). Some interpreters feel that these lines are out of place, and that they must originally have come earlier, for example, between verses 10 and 11. To place them elsewhere would, however, ruin the strong dramatic contrast they achieve in their present position as a preparation for chapter 30. It is not impossible, moreover, that the author, with different ideas of logical development from ours, intended just such a climax.

Although there are some difficulties in the translation of these verses, especially verse 24, the sense of the passage is clear. It presents Job as an honored speaker and leader. His decisions were final (vs. 22) and were always sought (vs. 23). He was not just a speaker, but was also skilled in leading the group.

The Contradiction of the Present (30:1-31)

"But now . . ." These words introduce a section which stands in total contrast to the preceding, just as Job's present condition contrasts with his former condition. The Hebrew phrase is repeated in verse 9 and in verse 16, making natural divisions of the chapter.

In suggesting the senseless horror of his present condition Job goes to the extreme. Where before he had enjoyed the honor and respect of the highest leaders, of princes and nobles, now he is the object of ridicule among the lowest classes, the dregs of humanity. From the standpoint of democratic and even humanitarian ideals the poet's words here have always seemed shocking. His description of men who were not worthy to be "set with the dogs" of Job's flock, whose strength and vigor have been reduced by hunger and want, who can be named only as "a senseless, a disreputable brood," is neither kind nor altogether in harmony with Job's earlier or later protestations of social responsibility. But it is not inconceivable that such a bitter word picture might have been drawn as appropriate to Job's feeling of alienation and to serve as a definitive proof of the absolute reversal of his fortunes. At any rate, the sight of Job here, the honorable man despised by his inferiors, the once wealthy man treated contemptuously by those who must eat the wild grasses, the respectable chieftain an object of sport among those who themselves have been driven out of society's limits—this sight confirms as perhaps no other in the book the depths of Job's condition and its seeming irrationality.

In another outburst Job continues his lament over his changed condition, but whereas in the preceding verses he has concen- trated on the character of his tormentors, here he dwells on the effect of their torment on him. An indication of the depth of his agony is to be found in verse 11, where it is plain that the ignoble and irreligious do not hesitate to regard Job as himself the object of God's punitive wrath. They do not hesitate, moreover, to in- crease their fury and their hostility against him, since obviously his greater misery must indicate that here at least is someone worse in the sight of God than they. They can judge him forsaken and perhaps find some measure of comfort for their true guilt. Once again there is a reminder of the New Testament where the One who was truly righteous was rejected by and tormented by evil men. Once again, too, the contrast is greater than the com- parison, for over against Job's understandable but bitter denuncia- tion of his tormentors must be placed the prayer of our Lord: "Father, forgive them; for they know not what they do" (Luke 23:34).

Finally, in verses 16-31 Job turns to the familiar burden of his complaint—the actual misery and suffering he endures, all the more unendurable because it so violently contrasts with his former happiness and prosperity (ch. 29).

This speech parallels in many details what Job has said else- where, but for its poignancy it remains the classic statement of his actual condition. Some of the language is difficult to translate (indicated by the marginal notes in the Revised Standard Ver- sion). But the general lines are clear: here is one who suffers days of affliction and nights of racking pain, one who finds no present help and comfort from God, one who faces a death which must be regarded in the eyes of the world as total defeat and con- demnation, one who still piteously cries for help which does not come, one whose expected fortune has become an irrational fate. The closing lines (vss. 28-31) sum up the desolation he feels as he recalls the ravages of his disease, his isolation from all men, and the fact that his only word can be one of mourning.

Job's Cry of "Innocent!" (31:1-40)

In chapter 31 the image of the courtroom is complete, for here Job, after having carefully reviewed the evidence in the case he is presenting, after having drawn the clear, unrelieved contrast between his former condition of righteousness and prosperity and his present condition of misery, now states his final argument. Thus "the words of Job are ended" (vs. 40), and save for two brief responses, he has nothing more to say on his own (40:3-5; 42:1-6).

This final plea is simply a declaration of innocence, in greater detail than he has given before. In the empty courtroom, desperately aware that his words are echoing in a void, he nevertheless plays the role of self-defense to the end. By the current standards and ways of viewing God's relationship to man, there could be only one explanation of the total reversal of Job's fortunes as set forth in chapters 29 and 30. That explanation is the one the friends have presented so ably and so consistently: that Job's sin has brought the inevitable retribution. In general terms Job has all along indignantly rejected this as a possible explanation in his case. Now he comes to particulars, and one after another he reels off the sins or transgressions that could be named against him. It is as though he leafs through a lawbook dealing with the possible infractions of an absolute code. As he reads, to each conceivable indictment he cries, "Innocent!" It is essential to remember that he does *not* know what crime is charged against him, he must make guess after guess.

The list makes an impressive speech. Some of the items Job mentions are the same that Eliphaz has guessed at shortly before (see 22:1-11), but Job is more exhaustive in his list than was Eliphaz. The list, moreover, is not arranged according to conventional standards of logical development, degrees of seriousness, or climactic order. This could mean that the speech has been disarranged (as many interpreters believe) but more probably that it reflects the desperation that Job feels and the fact that modern conceptions of orderly development and climactic arrangement are not the same as the literary standards which, in a different culture, guided the ancient composer of the Book of Job.

The Revised Standard Version has arranged the translation in convenient divisions, but the separate possibilities Job considers are indicated, not by these divisions, but by the recurrent form:

"if" followed by a possible transgression and the punishment or consequence which should properly have accompanied it (see vss. 5, 7, 9, and throughout the chapter).

Verses 1-4 are not phrased in the usual formula. They deal with the particular sin of sexual impurity (vss. 1-2) and with the more general matter of retribution that befalls all workers of evil. It is significant that Job not only declares by implication his innocence from overt acts of impurity, but even testifies that he has abstained from the intent to stimulate improper desire (see Matt. 5:28). That he goes further and states strongly the doctrine of retribution for sin need not surprise us. Although he has earlier raised the question whether *any* such moral order operates in the world (see especially 9:22-24), the book represents him as modifying these earlier excesses (see ch. 27, if it be the speech of Job), and certainly he must adopt the view as a hypothesis since it is the only one at hand. He has no other principle with which to work.

Verses 5 and 6 declare Job's innocence so far as falsehood is concerned. The modern reader cannot fail to be impressed by the high ethical quality of this chapter and by the way in which the hero again and again moves from the overt activity to the root of such activity in underlying attitudes. Verses 7 and 8 are rather general and may refer either to injustice or to uncleanness of lip and thought. The latter is probable since the next matter Job considers is adultery (vss. 9-12), a sin which he regards as particularly heinous (see the consequences in vss. 11-12).

In verses 13-15 there is a simple and beautiful declaration. If it is at odds with other words of Job's which seem to betray an insensitivity to the needs of some (see 30:1-8), this statement must be taken as his best view. The basis for simple justice in dealing with his servants is that fundamentally he, the master, and they, the servants, are alike the creations of the one God— an insight which was more urgently stressed in the Hebraic faith than in any other religion of antiquity, and one which is still far short of perfect realization.

The matter of justice between man and man, especially between the powerful and the poor, is pursued in verses 16-23. As Job recalls his past life he can find no occasion on which he has taken advantage of the weak, or has failed to extend positive charity. Verse 18 is difficult, but probably refers again to the common lot the needy and the wealthy share as children of one

Father. In verse 21 the phrase "help in the gate" refers to the possibility of getting a favorable decision for unjust acts; even with this legal right Job did not push an unfair or unjust advantage against such helpless ones as "the poor," "the widow," and "the fatherless."

The next section (vss. 24-28) deals not with social injustice but with the general sin of idolatry. This may be either the basic kind of idolatry, where gold, or any value, is made the primary confidence of life (vss. 24-25), or the more overt kind exemplified by the worship of sun and moon. The phrase "my mouth has kissed my hand" probably refers to an act of worship, perhaps secretly practiced.

Job further declares his innocence in the realm of inward attitude as he protests that he has been free even from joy over the ruin of an enemy (vss. 29-30; see the contrast to the attitude of some of the Imprecatory Psalms). He returns to the subject of his consistent practice of charity and adds the practice of hospitality (vss. 31-32). Again dealing with inner attitude, he even protests that, unlike Adam (vs. 33, see margin), or more probably unlike the mass of men—including us all—he has not concealed his sin.

Job has not concealed his sin because, as this speech makes increasingly clear, he is not conscious of sin. That fact comes to full statement in verses 35-37, where he sums up. Aware of his isolation and pathetically afraid that his speech and his testimony of innocence will go unheard, he nevertheless draws up the testimony and signs it. The word "signature" is actually "my taw," the last letter in the Hebrew alphabet. This, written as a kind of crossmark, could be a type of signature which Job imaginatively affixes to the symbolic document he has been drawing up to witness to his innocence (see a similar use of the image of writing in another climactic statement at 19:23-26). More probably it refers to the last words in his argument—as we would use "Z" or "Omega" as a symbol of conclusion.

Job has drawn up every conceivable indictment against himself and has rejected each one. If there is any other, even the indictment written by his "adversary," he still has no fear of being justifiably pronounced guilty. It is not clear whether by "adversary" Job means merely an enemy who would be eager to find falsity in him, or God. The lines in verses 36-37 seem to suggest the latter, for they depict Job as unafraid and resolute, taking

whatever charge could be brought against him, and turning it
from an adverse criticism or indictment into an occasion of pride
and glory. He can without fear or evasion "give him [God] an
account of all . . . [his] steps" and even approach the Almighty
"like a prince."

After this notable declaration the concluding verses (38-40)
sound lame and anticlimactic. There is, however, no sufficient
reason to rearrange them in a spot earlier in the chapter, for
what seems anticlimactic to us may have been a deliberate literary
device in another age with other standards of aesthetic enjoyment.
It is conceivable that the author intended for the speech to end
with this kind of trailing-off conclusion or reflective afterthought.
There is certainly a parallel to this in the conclusion of Job's
great speech in chapter 19. In this particular instance Job enters
a final cry of "Innocent!" almost as though it were uttered as he
stepped down from the witness stand. He is innocent of the
double sin of misusing the earth to the extent that its barren and
wasted fields could testify to his greed, or of reaping its produce
without balancing payment of labor.

To look back on the chapter as a whole, and especially on
the central affirmation in verses 35-37, is to be impressed with the
clarity of this picture. Here the poet presents his hero as the
righteous man who is secure in the awareness of his own righteousness. To say that he is "self-righteous" is not quite true, for
the term generally indicates the sin of pride. There is no hint that
the poet means this, or that he regards pride as the subtle sin
which must, in the end, be taken as the explanation of Job's
pain. No, here is the man whom God himself in the Prologue has
called "blameless and upright" (1:8). The picture is not meant
to repel. It is presented for approval, and its protestations are
nowhere denied. It is a true picture of Job, Job the righteous, the
perfect example of the Old Testament righteousness for which
the Law gave incentive and direction. As long as man's righteousness is measured by his fellow man or by Law, this must stand as
a testimony to a perfect man. It is when man stands before the
perfect God and finds himself measured not by Law but by what
God is, that this picture falls in ruins. Job can go no further until
he meets that God. We can go no further until we meet him in
Job's experience, or better in Jesus Christ.

THE SPEECHES OF ELIHU

Job 32:1—37:24

Introduction (32:1-5)

A glance at the format of verses 1-5 of chapter 32 in the Revised Standard Version shows that here a striking break in the Book of Job is reached, a fact which is confirmed strongly by the content of these verses. The section is in prose, like an island surrounded by a sea of poetry. Moreover, these verses introduce a new character into the discussion, one "Elihu the son of Barachel the Buzite, of the family of Ram." It is often pointed out by interpreters of the book that since Elihu is not mentioned in the Prologue his presence here seems suspiciously like an afterthought, and even an afterthought by someone other than the original author. It has similarly been pointed out that Elihu's contributions are not completely in harmony with the apparent intent of the author, and in fact appear at times to be an attempt to correct some of the excesses of the former discussion.

It must be said that, at least from the standpoint of contemporary literary standards, the conclusion is justifiable. But it must be realized too that practically all of the arguments against regarding Elihu's words as the work of the original author *are* arguments based on modern views of literary structure, dramatic effect, and climactic order. All of these considerations are in the end matters of taste, and one must be hesitant about imposing standards of taste, especially modern ones, upon the creations of antiquity. One could affirm, with justice, that Elihu was not mentioned in the Prologue because he was not part of the original story used by the author as dramatic background, but that the author deliberately held him in reserve for dramatic effect, intending to present some of his own theological positions through this new mouth.

Similarly one could say that, although to Western and modern ears, tutored by Greek and Shakespearean notions of drama, the intervention of Elihu dulls the sharp effect achieved by placing the speeches of the Almighty next to the closing words of Job, this may be a deliberate device. It is conceivable that the intent was to provide a literary transition from the discussion to the closing speeches.

At a deeper level it is possible to argue that the words of Elihu form a kind of logical climax to the discussion itself. It has been pointed out before that, particularly near the close, the drama assumes more and more the character of a courtroom proceeding. The closing speech of Job (chs. 28 ?, 29-31) may be likened to a summation of Job's point of view, presented in less passionate terms than before. In Elihu the excessive and exaggerated statements of the friends appear in more reflective fashion, and, indeed, in his words one finds the best that can be said for the view that there is *some* meaning in *some* suffering. And this, in the end, is what Elihu with all his own eccentric mannerisms seems to be saying. That it is also the viewpoint of the original author is possible and even probable.

The new speaker carries a familiar name, Elihu, meaning "He is my God" (see, for example, I Sam. 1:1 and I Chron. 27:18; for "Buzite" see Gen. 22:21 and compare Job 1:1; and for "Ram" see Ruth 4:18-22, although the two names do not point to the same family or tribe).

The cause of Elihu's concern is twofold. First, there was Job's self-justification, or literally Job's determination to maintain his own righteousness in the presence of God (vs. 2). Second, there was the silence of the friends, which Elihu takes to be an admission of defeat (vs. 3).

The little prologue to Elihu's speeches supplies one additional fact: that Elihu was younger than the other participants in the discussion. This is used as explanation of his reticence in speaking, as his wrath is explanation of the breach of reticence. Elihu's youth is sometimes seen by interpreters as a kind of comic feature, and some have accordingly found comic values in his words. Again this is to judge the literary creation by contemporary standards. There is no suggestion that the author intended the youth of the speaker to be a humorous matter, and it is as easy to assume that he meant to indicate that here, at least, was one instance in which when youth spoke it showed greater wisdom than did age, particularly when age was bound by a paralyzed orthodoxy.

The First Speech (32:6—33:33)

Let Me Also Declare My Opinion (32:6—33:7)

In a long introductory statement Elihu justifies to the friends, who are presumably still present (32:6-14), to any nearby witnesses (32:15-22), and to Job (33:1-7), the fact that he now enters the discussion.

Elihu's justification, so far as Eliphaz, Bildad, and Zophar are concerned, is clearly that he feels they have been bested by Job. In deference to their greater age and therefore presumably greater wisdom he has waited. But, in his view, wisdom is not necessarily the virtue of age, for it comes from the "spirit" or "breath of the Almighty" in a man. Elihu here is completely in harmony with a basic position of the wisdom school, namely, that true wisdom, which belongs to God alone, can be achieved by man only by virtue of his "share" in the divine wisdom, the wisdom that brought him into being and still directs him. Underlying Elihu's words is a profound understanding of the Creation story, in which man comes to life in the image of God as God breathes into him "the breath of life" (Gen. 2:7), coupled with the concept of the creative and providential wisdom of God as found, for instance, in Proverbs 8. This "spirit" which is equivalent to "wisdom" Elihu claims as his own (see 32:18).

In a more negative way Elihu also condemns the three friends for their complete failure with Job. Verses 13 and 14 are somewhat difficult, although they must carry basically the same thought as verses 11 and 12. Verse 13 is certainly a warning to the friends not to think either that they have represented "wisdom" by their speeches or that they have discovered it in Job's. The last line may be a sarcastic reference to their conclusion that Job could not be defeated by man's arguments and that God must now "vanquish him." If so, then verse 14 is Elihu's insistence that what they have not been able to accomplish he will undertake, although the connection between the two lines of the verse is not clear.

In verses 15-22 the speaker turns away from the friends. He is represented as speaking to actual bystanders or perhaps better to himself, since an audience is generally not suggested in the poem. He declares that he cannot keep silence, that he is ready to burst with "the spirit" which gives him wisdom, and that he will show no personal bias in his words.

Finally, in the preamble to his contribution Elihu addresses Job directly (33:1-7). Again he justifies his words by an appeal to his possession of the divine creative spirit of wisdom (33:4). But more especially he speaks to Job's former appeals. Job has previously bewailed the fact that God "is not a man" as he himself is, and therefore he has begged that God "take his rod away" and "let not dread of him terrify" (9:32-34). The latter plea was reiterated in 13:21. To this complaint Elihu now offers himself in answer. Elihu is not the strange and unapproachable God, but a man as Job is, "toward God" in the same way, made also "from a piece of clay." He therefore will not terrify and his "pressure" (or more probably, with the Greek translation, "hand," see also 13:21) will not be "heavy" upon Job. It is possible that Elihu means to offer his services as the "umpire" for whom Job has longed, the one who could represent both God and man. The truth is, however, that despite Elihu's claims, he represents only man and not God. In the end God must speak for himself.

God Does Speak to Man (33:8-33)

Job's contentions are seen by Elihu to be twofold. First, he has resolutely maintained his own innocence and the fact that God has irrationally afflicted him and has counted him to be an enemy rather than a friend (vss. 8-11; for parallels from Job's own words see 9:21; 13:24, 26-27; 16:17). Second, Job has denied that God answers man's questions or that God speaks to man at all (vs. 13; see 13:3, 22-24; 16:20-21; 19:7; 23:3-9). To the first Elihu answers in a pure negative (Job is "not right") and in a positive statement of the greatness of God (vs. 12).

To the second complaint Elihu gives more attention. Whereas Job has questioned whether God speaks at all, Elihu maintains that God does speak within the channel of man's own experience. It is not entirely clear whether by the "one" and "two" ways mentioned in verse 14 it is meant that there are literally *two* fashions of God's speaking, for this sort of numerical expression is common for "any number." But it is clear that Elihu does think of God as speaking to man in two ways: by a kind of dream vision and as a possible consequence of suffering.

The first way (33:15-18) has already been claimed by Eliphaz as his own experience (see 4:12-13), and can hardly have much interest for Job, who has declared that in his case the night brings no such reassuring word of revelation but only further distress and "visions" that terrify (7:13-14). But it is interesting that Elihu sees that the result of such divine "speaking" would be the ethical conversion of man, turning him from his evil ways and so "redeeming" him.

When he turns to the experience of suffering itself Elihu expands the subject and in the end gives a theory which is not unique but which is stated with considerable power. He does not declare that suffering itself is a means of God's speaking. The experience which Job undergoes is nowhere in the book laid at the door of God but, as in the Prologue, is seen to come from elsewhere. The experience is rather a kind of chastening preparation, by which man is made ready to hear the message of God.

In Elihu's description of suffering there is no question but that he draws the details from Job's own case, including the wasting of the body (see 19:20). The experience he treats is exactly parallel to that of Job, who has drawn near "the Pit." "Those who bring death" may be a reference to angels such as are mentioned in II Samuel 24:16 and Psalm 78:49. Against such a dark background the speaker now sketches the steps of the divine intervention. First there is "for him an angel" who is described as one of "the thousand" ministering spirits of God, and also as a "mediator" or "interpreter" (in the Hebrew). This is one who is both gracious to help and just "to declare to man what is right for him." He thus may bring to light man's true need and sin, but he also declares that he has "found a ransom" for him. As part of his ministry on behalf of the sufferer the "angel" intercedes for him, asking that he be delivered and restored to vigor.

Consequent to the activity of the "angel" on his behalf the suffering man now prays on his own part. When he is restored he also witnesses to men concerning the reason for his predicament and the grace of God in delivering him. Thus to his songs of salvation there will be added the praise of the congregation. A close parallel is to be found in Psalm 40:1-3, where there is the same progression of experience but without the activity of the angel who is mediator.

Finally Elihu again calls upon Job to consider his words (33: 29-33), and to know that God thus acts to speak to man; the purpose of God, he sees, is to bring a man to "see the light of life." If Job has any further arguments he is invited to give them or, failing that, to keep silence while Elihu proceeds. His desire to "justify" Job must be understood not as a desire to maintain Job's right against God but as a professed willingness to agree with Job if he has any worthwhile arguments to give.

Elihu's words in 33:19-28 must be taken as one of the great high points of the Old Testament revelation. Here dramatic imagery traces mankind's complete helplessness, facing only the prospect of death and final meaninglessness. To this despairing estimate there is given the opposing prospect of an angelic mediator, one who has "found" a ransom, one whose graciousness and whose righteousness fit him to stand as "interpreter" both of God and of man, who, moreover, intercedes in behalf of dying man. To say that we stand close to the New Testament here is obvious.

The Second Speech (34:1-37)

Job's Errors (34:1-9)

The phrase, "Then Elihu said," indicates that there is a break here (see also 35:1 and 36:1), and that we have the second of what are to be four distinct speeches. This one is addressed to the "wise men," who may be either the friends or, more probably, the imagined onlookers. They are invited to consider the argument that will be presented and to judge its truth by their reason.

The direction of Elihu's argument here is forecast by his quotation or interpretation of Job's former words. Job's errors, as they are enumerated by Elihu, are, first, to have declared his own "righteousness" (see, for example, 9:21; 13:18); second, at least by implication, to have asserted God's unrighteousness (see, for example, 9:22-31; 27:2); and third, to have maintained that religion brings no profit to man. The last charge cannot be substantiated by Job's speeches, but it clearly represents the drift of his thought in his exaggerated pictures of the prosperity that apparently rewards wickedness. It is interesting that Elihu's speech reflects some use of the Prologue, for the same idea is put interrogatively into the mouth of Satan there (1:9). These erroneous views place Job in the category of "evildoers" and "wicked men" (34:8), even though he may not have engaged in the kind of overt unrighteousness with which the friends have charged him.

The Truth of the Matter (34:10-37)

The third error Elihu leaves for the time being (but see ch. 35, where it is focal), and gives his primary attention to the double error of man's maintaining his own righteousness so as to impugn God's righteousness. Verses 12 and 23 may be thought of as the central thoughts in his argument, setting forth as two basic positions the absolute righteousness of God and the impossibility of bringing that righteousness into question.

These two ideas seem to be taken by Elihu as fundamental postulates, to which all reasonable men must agree. They are not greatly different from the positions the friends have previously affirmed. But there is a difference of approach. Job and the friends have both tried to establish or disprove the propositions on the basis of Job's particular case. Elihu somewhat clears the air, and returns to the principles which must stand even in face of apparent contradictions. As such he presents a finer picture than the friends and in many ways expresses some of the deepest truths of the book.

In verses 10-15 the thought is clear, namely, that the idea of God and the idea of wickedness are not compatible. Elihu does not go so far as to say that what God does would be right even though judged as wrong by human standards; rather, he maintains that the divine omnipotence and providence presuppose absolute right. Verses 14 and 15, building upon the story of the Creation, especially emphasize God's providential care and man's total dependence. Man, created from the dust by the gift of the divine Spirit, or breath, would cease to exist if God were to withdraw his Spirit or bring an end to his concern for man. Man's life, then, is wholly derivative, to be explained only in terms of his relationship to and dependence upon the creative and providential power of God (for the same picture see Eccles. 12:7).

God's righteousness is seen by Elihu to be particularly expressed in his suppression of wickedness in rulers and in his ordering of human events so that injustice is brought to an end (vss. 16-20). The view of God that is set forth is essentially that of a transcendent Being who remains in control of the world and who acts in a fashion consistent with his own righteousness but whose operations are actually obscure to man (vss. 21-28). This of course has been the root of Job's complaint, to which Elihu seems to be saying, "That is the way it is, and it cannot be otherwise." When God does *not* act as man thinks he should, he still cannot be questioned (vs. 29). The connection of verse 30 is not clear, and at other places in this section the meaning must be arrived at on the basis of conjecture or from the versions.

In verses 31-33 the apparent meaning is either that when God does not requite evil it is because of some secret conversion of the evildoer, or that if someone (Job) is threatened by punishment and demands to know his indictment he may not necessarily be answered exactly to his liking.

Elihu ends his second speech with a general appeal for agreement among those who are truly wise and with a direct charge of Job's wickedness. Agreeing with the friends here he finds in Job's protestations evidence of his guilt (we should say evidence of a "guilt complex"), but he also sees the protestations themselves as rebellion against the transcendent and omnipotent God whose picture he has just drawn.

The Third Speech (35:1-16)

In this, the shortest of the four divisions of Elihu's utterances, the speaker turns to the third charge of error he had previously brought against Job, that of declaring that religion was profitless to man (see 34:9). Here, however, Elihu clarifies the issue: it is that Job maintains that he has a *right to complain* to God that faithfulness has brought him no "advantage." It is this with which Elihu deals, not the question of whether there *is* any profit.

Elihu offers Job and his "friends" an answer to this complaint. Since it can hardly be said that Eliphaz, Bildad, and Zophar reflect Job's view here, the "friends" in this case must be any imagined supporters for his ideas. In fact, Elihu is close to Eliphaz (compare 22:2-3 with 35:2-8) when he declares that man does *not* have the right to press the question of advantage of righteousness since neither man's righteousness nor his wickedness affects God. Transgressions do not diminish him, nor do pious acts give him anything. Man's morality does affect mankind but not the transcendent God. Again Elihu is seen to be arguing from the very idea of God, and warning against any tendency to construct a God out of the materials of man's reason or his experiences. In so doing he comes close, of course, to viewing God as so removed from human life that he cannot be known—or loved—at all. And in one sense at least there stands against Elihu, as the other side of the truth he sets forth, the whole incredible fact of the Cross of Jesus Christ, with its manifestation of how far man's unrighteousness *does* affect God.

When Elihu turns to the seemingly contradictory aspects of Job's own case, he has an original solution to offer. When men do cry to God because of their sufferings, as Job has been doing, it is because of the suffering and not because of a true desire for God.

In his very cry for relief man remains centered in himself, and not in his Creator. Verses 10 and 11 are reminiscent of the Garden of Eden where man was made superior to the beasts of the earth and the birds of the air, to have dominion over them and to live as the image of the Maker. In his experiences, however, man is determinedly self-centered and does not seek for God, who alone can transform the night of suffering with songs of deliverance (see 33:26-28). Thus, although men like Job complain, they are not answered, because even their cry is another symptom of the evil disease of pride (vss. 12-13).

Job's insistence, then, that he has a case and that he waits for God's answer must in the end be seen as arrogance. In fact, Elihu declares that *because* God has not answered, Job is bold to push his complaint to even greater extremes (vss. 15 and 16, but the meaning is not certain; see margin). Elihu certainly sees the issues on a more profound level than have the friends, although his diagnosis is not flawless. In the ultimate resolution of the book, Job is not condemned for this sin of pride which Elihu posits. But it can be credited to Elihu's account that he steadfastly avoids the trap of declaring that Job's tragedy is due specifically to this or any other sin, and that his view of God is a positive preparation for the coming speeches of the Almighty.

The Fourth Speech (36:1—37:24)

The two values of Elihu's speeches mentioned above come to clearest recognition in his concluding speech. Here it seems that the poet is concerned to establish the fact that suffering, though not *caused* by God, can be used by him (36:1-25), and to provide a skillful introduction (36:26—37:24) for the overwhelmingly powerful speeches of the Almighty.

The Almighty Will Not Pervert Justice (36:1-25)

In a short preface to the speech Elihu claims again the attention of Job, promising to bring extensive knowledge (so probably the meaning of "from afar" in vs. 3), and declaring his own intention to keep steadfastly to the principle he has before enunciated: that God's righteousness is absolute. His statement that one "perfect in knowledge" (vs. 4) was present is probably not a bit of self-conscious pride but a reference to God who alone knows all (see the same expression in 37:16).

The key to the first part of the speech is verse 5, paralleling the key to the second part in verse 26. Elihu draws two conclusions from the power of God. The first is that he "does not despise any." Here is the corrective to what might otherwise seem a coldness and heartlessness in Elihu's theology. He affirms that God retains active control of the world of men, particularly in establishing the righteous (vs. 7).

Against such a view there still stands, of course, the contradictory evidence of Job's tragic case. To answer it Elihu returns to the principle that suffering and affliction are the means whereby God educates his own, calling them through such experiences away from arrogance and transgression, and bestowing prosperity and length of life upon the penitent (vss. 8-12). It should be noted that Elihu still does not directly charge God with *causing* the affliction, again reflecting the point of view of the Prologue.

Verses 13 and 14 deal with the opposite principle, that of retribution on the wicked, for whom affliction becomes an occasion for added anger and indifference to God. These die untimely and shameful deaths (see margin of vs. 14).

Job still halts between the two possibilities. Elihu warns him not to let himself be enticed into yet more grievous sinning by the suffering he undergoes. Here again he reflects more clearly the issues of the Prologue than those of the ensuing discussion, for his advice is parallel to Job's initial reaction: "Shall we receive good at the hand of God, and shall we not receive evil?" (2:10).

Verse 16 introduces a very difficult passage. The main questions are these: How can Job's former prosperity ("broad place," "table . . . full of fatness") be regarded as an "allurement" of Job by God? Does the first line of verse 17 mean that Job suffers the judgment on the wicked, or that formerly he himself casually condemned others as wicked, or that he now shares in the judgment which wicked men express against God? The meaning of the second line will depend on the selection of a rendering for the first. In verse 18 does the "greatness of the ransom" refer to the extreme cost of restoration in Job's submission to an imaginary indictment? In the face of these and other questions that can be raised and for which no absolutely certain answer can be found on the basis of the word meanings, we may say only that Elihu here warns Job against the dangers of further revolt and counsels a kind of submission. Beyond this we may not go, and it is not clear to what Job is to submit.

At verse 21 the meaning becomes clearer, and the translation of the Revised Standard Version reveals the sense. The passage closes with advice, both negative and positive. Negatively Job should remember that God's lessons must be assumed to be right; positively he should fix his attention on the mighty works of God in the past.

The Almighty Cannot Be Known (36:26—37:24)

Here is the second conclusion Elihu draws from the power of God: "We know him not." Verse 26 parallels verse 5; they are alike in form and balance each other. The passage that begins here and continues through chapter 37 is also a striking literary introduction to the speeches of the Lord and to the content of the first one of these.

One should not miss also the significance of Elihu's root idea, as his words are brought to a close by the storm. "We do not know him" is a judgment that is on firmer ground than either Job or the friends hold, if chapter 28 be excepted. In their separate ways they have agreed on the fact that God can be known by the exercise of man's reason, or—as would be truer to the Hebrew way of thinking—on the basis of man's experience. Job and the friends disagree about the meaning of his experience, but they agree that it has some relationship to the knowledge of God. Elihu startlingly lifts the focus of attention away from Job to the magnificent and mysterious elements of creation, almost as though to demand that the fury and splendor of a storm be set alongside Job's case as part of the materials from which the knowledge of God must be derived.

Among the natural phenomena to which Elihu points as confirmation for his position, as stated in 36:26, are the refreshing rain (vss. 27-28, the language of which is reminiscent of the Garden of Eden), and the clouds and the lightning which bring either destructive judgment or productive blessings (vss. 29-33). The phrase "the roots of the sea" is strange, and has been translated by some, with a slight textual change, "he covers the sun by day."

In chapter 37 Elihu continues to point to the inexplicable and powerful activity of God in nature, always regarding the natural events as not "natural" at all but "supernatural," but always stressing that they are God's events. Verses 1-5 elaborate the picture of the storm, and verses 6-10 deal with new evidences, the ice, snow, and cold of winter. The first line of verse 7 refers to the fact that the inclement weather forces man to be inactive. The second line probably means, as in the margin, that man, the workmanship of God, comes to recognize his own created nature when he thus feels the effects of God's working in the world.

Verses 11 and 12 return to the theme of the storm, especially the movements of the clouds. Then verse 13 takes up the last part of the preceding verse and stresses the fact that this is God's activity, bringing about his own purpose, whether to be corrective or to reveal his love (the phrase "or for his land" may be out of place, since it upsets the balance of the lines).

One more feature remains in Elihu's recounting of the wonders of nature—the oppressive heat of summer, when the air is still, the garments hang hotly on the body, and the sky is spread out like a brassy and glaring mirror (vss. 14-18). While he declares this wonder Elihu also makes a pointed appeal to Job to consider all this (vss. 14, 19-20). The "darkness" of verse 19 is the darkness of man's understanding, therefore Elihu cannot imagine *desiring* to speak to this Almighty God, for it would be equivalent to self-destruction (vs. 20).

Although there are some difficulties in verses 21-24, it is likely that they form the final transition to the speeches of the Lord in chapters 38-41. Thus they seem to indicate the coming of a brightness after the storm, and the presence of God in golden splendor. In the after effects of the storm we are prepared for hearing the voice of the Almighty whom "we cannot find" but who himself speaks to Job. Verses 23 and 24 return to the theological theme of Elihu's whole set of speeches: that God is infinitely great and righteous, and does not himself violate the principle of righteousness in dealing with men. His righteousness, therefore, is unimpeachable; it is not to be called into question but is to become the basis for godly fear in men. A sounder prelude to the content of the speeches of the Lord and their effect on Job could hardly be imagined.

THE SPEECHES OF THE LORD
Job 38:1—42:6

The Book of Job, set within the framework of a story Prologue and Epilogue, reaches its conclusion in a series of discourses placed by the author in the mouth of God himself. It is correct to say that it is "conclusion" rather than "climax." The latter term,

which is often used to describe these speeches, like an alternate
term "denouement" carries too much the sense of literary development according to contemporary standards. The problem in regarding these speeches as a climax to the book, moreover, is that they simply do not include climactic material. We
come to them with a high sense of expectancy and often are dis-
appointed. We look for a final answer to the questions that have
swarmed perplexingly in the discussion and there are no answers
here. Elihu gives far more solutions than does the Lord.

This is not to say that the speeches are lacking in content or
significance. But the meaning is to be found along two lines: first,
not in what God says but in that he speaks at all, and second, in
that he poses questions rather than gives answers.

The structure of the speeches is fairly simple. First, following
an introductory summons (38:1-3) there is a series of questions
drawn from the order of creation, including natural phenomena
and animal life (38:4—40:2). To this Job makes short answer
(40:3-5). There follows another speech, with its own introductory summons (40:6-14), dealing with two matters of evidence,
Behemoth and Leviathan (40:15—41:34). To this Job again
gives answer (42:1-6).

Introductory Summons (38:1-3)

The poet now brings into the discussion the last participant,
who has the final word. It is "the LORD," named with the ancient
name which carries overtones of Covenant relationship and love.
The Lord "answered" Job out of the storm ("whirlwind"). As
indicated in the comment on chapter 37, it is conceivable that the
author meant the reader to imagine a great storm approaching, at
the end of which, rather than in its midst, God speaks. It is not
amiss, then, to say that the words of the Lord begin *after* the
storm of the discussion, and are somewhat parallel to the "still
small voice" of Elijah's experience (I Kings 19:12). At any rate,
it is not necessary to imagine the following speech shouted over
the thundering of a storm.

Job has repeatedly demanded a hearing with God (see 13:3,
22; 23:3-9). The tables are now turned, for God demands a hearing. God speaks, but speaks to ask his own questions. The first of
these questions points to the confusion caused by the recent discussion. "Who is this . . . ?" may refer to Job, rather than to

Elihu, since the following verse is plainly addressed to Job. For this reason many feel that Elihu's speeches are a later addition and that the words of the Lord were originally placed just after Job's closing words in chapter 31. It must be granted that the effect would be dramatic, but it should also be said that the logical connection is not so strong as in the present arrangement. Moreover, it is not impossible that the first question of the Lord refers to Elihu. Certainly the question condemns all of the discussion which has confused the fact that there is a "counsel" or purpose in God's ordering of life. Job has given the alternatives: either let God question and he will answer, or let him speak and God answer. The Lord chooses the first and calls Job to a contest of strength, addressing him as a "hero" (a more literal translation than "man") who wishes to enter argument with the Divine.

The Wonders of Creation (38:4—40:2)

The regular strophic structure of the English translation in the Revised Standard Version reflects the generally even measures of the poem as it unfolds, pointing, one after the other, to the majestic mysteries of creation. It was perhaps typical of the times that in the last century these elements of creation were often regarded as rational evidences of God's existence and rule. Of course the opposite is true: they are not proofs which will convince Job's reason; they are demonstrations in the physical sphere of the limitations of his reason, the multiplicity of mystery which meets him on every side. It is interesting to contrast these chapters with Job's avowal of innocence in chapter 31. There he lists the evidence as he sees it: his own experience. Here God opens the doors on a mass of evidence which cannot be controlled by man.

The list begins with the most general evidence, that is, the fact of creation itself (38:4-7). The image is that of the architect's construction (see the parallel in Prov. 8:22-31, where the "wisdom" of God is the architectural workman). Job's assumption that he has wisdom is refuted by the fact that he was not present when "wisdom" wrought its principles into the structure of the world. Although "the morning stars" and "the sons of God" (here angelic beings) saluted the birth of creation with songs of joy and praise, Job was not there (compare the angelic song at the moment when the new creation is born, Luke 2:13-14).

In close connection with the general structure of creation there is cited God's control of "the sea" (vss. 8-11). The imagery is partly to be explained on the basis of the physical sea, always to the Hebrew a symbol of restlessness and dark power, but partly also on the basis of the ancient cosmology in which "the sea" represented the chaotic forces "under the firmament" and "above the firmament" (Gen. 1:6-7), forces which, if unrestrained, could break out in a kind of demonic power to destroy. It is thus of the greatest importance that God should prescribe "bounds for it" and give it a limiting command (see also the individual parallel in God's limitation on the work of the Satan in Job 1:12 and 2:6).

The third aspect of creation's mysteries is the regular return of the dawn, which with its rays casts deep impressions of shadows and turns the earth red (vs. 14). In a powerful image the morning is also seen as shaking out the earth as a cloth is shaken, dispossessing the wicked of their cover of darkness and so breaking "their uplifted arm" or bringing their nocturnal purposes to failure (vss. 13 and 15).

The next figure (vss. 16-18) brings us again to the ancient cosmology, and questions Job concerning his knowledge of things beneath the surface. Does he understand the hidden springs which feed the waters of the earth, does he know anything of Sheol, the place of the dead, or does he even comprehend the fullness of the earth, "all" that God had made? (Gen. 1:31).

In a further reference to the initial act of creation the Lord asks about Job's knowledge of the origin of light and darkness and of the way to their separate dwellings (vss. 19-20; compare Gen. 1:3-4). The ironic flavor of the questions and challenges in these speeches is particularly evident in verse 21.

Snow and hail are the subjects of the next questions (vss. 22-24). These are thought of poetically as stored up in reserve for God's use, especially in "the time of trouble." The latter phrase must refer to the effect of hail and snow in turning back Israel's enemies (see Joshua 10:11; Ps. 68:14). Verse 24 seems to break the pattern, although "light" may be understood as "lightning," in which case it and "the east wind" would continue the subject of storms.

In the next section (vss. 25-27), where rain is the subject, the term "channel" refers to an open sluiceway from heaven, not to a channel upon earth. The wonder in view is the extraordinary power of a heavy rainfall, and the apparently indiscriminate way the blessings of the rain are distributed. To point to the effect of rain upon a "waste and desolate land" where "there is no man" is at least to remind Job that there are in creation evidences of God's working and control beyond his knowledge and which are not to be understood in terms of *human* values.

Several phenomena are grouped in verses 28-30. Job is asked whether he can determine the origin of rain or dew or frost, and whether he can understand such a remarkable feature as ice, when "the waters become hard like stone." Ice was, of course, scarce in the region of Palestine, so that the report of it by travelers or its rare occurrence would be the occasion for marvel.

Job is then queried with reference to the constellations (vss. 31-33), in particular whether he has power to control or even to understand their orderly movements. "The chains of the Pleiades" is a difficult phrase, possibly referring to the grouping of stars which we know by that name (see also Amos 5:8; Job 9:9), but perhaps to some group which seemed to remain constant while "Orion" moved; "the Mazzaroth" and "the Bear" are also probably to be understood as constellations, since the context seems to call for such a meaning. The identification of these various heavenly bodies is not as certain as the English terms "Bear" and "Orion" suggest.

In the last of the references to physical phenomena, the subject of storms and rain is again taken up (vss. 34-38). Job is queried as to his ability to control the rain, which according to the poetic figure is summoned by the voice of God (vs. 34). Similarly a question reveals to him the vast difference between his power and understanding and the power and understanding of God, for whom the lightning acts as an obedient servant (vs. 35). Two key words in verse 36 are difficult to translate (see margin). The Revised Standard Version, by its rendering, preserves the figure of the rain and storm, although the idea that clouds and mist act in somewhat independent wisdom is not altogether in accord with the context. Verse 37 returns to the theme of God's control of the forces of nature, especially in the strong image of the rain poured out of heaven as from a container in such profusion that the normally dry land is turned to mud.

From the manifold mysteries of the heavens and the earth which have been described in such powerful fashion, the poet turns to the equally mysterious and incomprehensible world of animal life (38:39—39:30). In reducing the scope of the subject he is by no means changing it. Here is the same exuberant marveling before infinite mystery; here is the same deep interest in natural phenomena; and here is the same basic conviction that characterizes the whole speech of the Lord, namely, that in the presence of the order of creation man discovers such boundaries and limits to his reason that he cannot presume to understand the ways of the Almighty, much less call him to account. In the catalogue of illustrations that follows, the primary criterion of selection seems to be the vast irrationality of elements within creation, elements which do not perform at all according to the standards of human reason.

The first question in this group is the most general: whether Job, who has assumed that he has sufficient knowledge to question the Almighty, actually has enough knowledge to carry on a minor part of nature's services. Can he provide for the young of beast or bird, as God himself does? (See also Psalm 104:21 and Jesus' words concerning God's care for his creatures in Matthew 6:26.) The combination of "lion" and "raven" is striking and may be a deliberate desire to cover the whole range of animal life. It has been suggested, however, that the word translated "for the raven" could be rendered "at evening," keeping the single example of the lion (see the parallel in Ps. 104:20-22).

In 39:1-4 the Lord again points to Job's ignorance, this time with reference to the habits of "mountain goats" and "hinds." They act independently of man, who does not have to exercise control over them. The phrase, "can you number," probably means "can you determine the number of," referring not to the lapse of time from conception to birth but to Job's powerlessness in determining the processes of birth.

Verses 5-8 constitute a dramatic picture of "the wild ass," living in freedom in the wilderness. The point of the image is of course the fact that here is a creature that serves no useful purpose ("he hears not the shouts of the driver"), and so must seem to be an unintelligible part of creation. At least man is not able easily to categorize such elements in God's world.

Similarly, and even more pointedly, the Lord points Job to "the wild ox" (vss. 9-12; the term was once, through the influence of the Greek translation, wrongly rendered "unicorn"). Once again we are brought face to face with creation in its unintelligibility, for man would not be able to explain satisfactorily *why* such creatures exist and *why* such power is expended in vain.

The unintelligible and even irrational side of creation surely comes to focus in the figure of "the ostrich" (vss. 13-18), and the description here emphasizes what is erratic in its behavior. The verses are absent in the Greek translation, but in general they are faithful to the sense of this section (but see the third-person mention of "God" in verse 17). The reference is to the fact that the eggs are often left unguarded before the time of brooding, and to the general ungainliness of the bird itself. Again there appears the incongruity of great strength and speed in such a creature (vs. 18, although the first line includes a conjecture).

The most extended image appears in verses 19-25, where the poet draws a dramatic picture of "the horse." The particular meaning of the image here is the extraordinary behavior of the horse in war. By implication it is clear that Job did not so order things, nor can he ever give a rational explanation of such strange activity and such apparently prodigal strength in an animal.

Verses 26-30 seem rather anticlimactic after the drama of the preceding verses, but the ancient poet apparently did not conceive of climactic effect as we do. This first speech of the Lord ends with a fleeting reminder of such inexplicable elements in creation as the migration of a bird and the presence in the world and habits of a predatory bird like the eagle (see the parallel to the last line of vs. 30 in Matt. 24:28).

In preparation for the response of Job there is now a repetition of the questions with which the speech of the Lord began. Job is asked in effect if he wishes to go further with the argument, or whether he wishes to yield (so probably the meaning of the first line of 40:2).

The Response of Job (40:3-5)

To the evidence that has been offered, Job has no answer. In effect he does "yield," at least to the point established by the foregoing speech: namely, that in view of all the incomprehensibility around him he is "of small account." There is more to come, but at least at this point one may say that Job has changed orientation. Formerly he has insisted that *his* reasons take priority and that he be regarded as a central issue in God's rule. Upon his case, he has insisted, the righteousness of God must be made to depend. Now the scene has shifted until he and his evidence are on the edge of a great circle of evidence, too vast to comprehend but which must ultimately be included in any attack on or any justification of the ways of God. It should not be forgotten that if the evidence just cited by the Lord contraverts Job's attempt to define too narrowly the elements by which one comes to know God, it far more contradicts the little confidences of the friends who believe that they have arrived at a definition of God's righteousness on the basis of human experience.

Behemoth and Leviathan (40:6—41:34)

Introductory Summons (40:6-14)

After Job's answer, which, it must be admitted, is partial and relatively noncommital, the Book of Job represents the Lord as marshaling still more evidence to be considered in the case at hand. This second speech is often regarded by interpreters as not a part of the original work, the main reasons being found in the content and in the somewhat altered style. Certainly there is a major difference: where the former evidences have been cited in sharp and brief allusions, these two pictures of Behemoth and Leviathan are extraordinarily detailed and contain exaggerated features. It is entirely possible that they include parts of poetic pictures of these beasts, composed before the writing of the Book of Job, or even after it. In the first case they could have been utilized by the author, as perhaps he used the poem on wisdom in chapter 28; in the latter case they would, of course, have been inserted by later editors who found them consonant with the original work.

At the same time, it should be stressed that *something* belongs here. Job's confession in 40:2-5 is by no means complete and we cannot conceive of an ending to the book at this point. Moreover, this speech is introduced in a strongly repetitious way, with 40:6-7 practically paralleling 38:1-3. It would be incredible if some later editor would have thus repeated; one can only assume that the original author intended the two speeches to stand as parallel evidences, the first pointing to the remarkable and non-classifiable features of the natural world, the second to two isolated instances which also have some overtones of ancient mythology, and which therefore suit the author's purpose of stressing God's power. For the author of Job, the mythological features are of course only poetic expressions.

The question stated in parallel in verse 8 brings us to the central issue, which is not so much the impropriety of *bringing* a case to God as the underlying intent of such action, conscious or no, which is to "deny" or "make ineffectual" the justice or righteous rule of God. Job, it must be remembered, could find no reason within the usual standards of human righteousness to call himself "unrighteous." By maintaining his own righteousness as unimpeachable he must necessarily impeach the righteousness of God. To "justify" himself he must "condemn" God. Here is a classic view of man in any attempt at self-justification, whether to himself or to his neighbor or to his God. Job could be *justified by God* (so in the Prologue) and God could himself still be just, but if Job must have the security of being assured of his righteousness by mechanical or rational proofs then he must ever be in the position of condemning God. Only by accepting the verdict of God— and such a verdict must be accepted on the basis of faith—could Job come to any resolution of his problem.

Verses 9-14 prepare for the culmination of the Lord's address to Job. It is an ironic challenge to Job to assume control of the world, to express his "anger" in righteous judgments on the wicked, to dispense justice in absolute rectitude. When he has so done—that is, when he has reordered the world to conform to his own principles and standards, and has done so rightly—then God himself will "acknowledge" him. God will accept Job's own self-estimate. But the original goes deeper here. The literal meaning of the verb in the first line of verse 14 is "praise," the word normally being used of man's worship of God. If Job can do what he is challenged to do—and what implicitly his argument has assumed he can do—then he will *be* God. The ancient sin of the pair in the Garden, with their attempt to be "like God" (Gen. 3:5), is here seen to be Job's. Every effort at self-justification must ultimately stand under the same condemnation.

Behold Behemoth (40:15-24)

The general features of the description and the Egyptian setting ("lotus plants," "the river") make it clear that the animal here described is a hippopotamus. At the same time certain other features, such as the exaggerations and the phrase "the first of the works of God," bring to mind a mythological beast. It is possible that the author meant both, and used the actual, and strange, Egyptian animal to typify the extraordinary and superhuman elements in creation which, no less than the familiar animals of chapter 39, are under the control of God. The point of the first speech was Job's inability to *understand,* and the evidence was drawn from the vast and irrational elements of the world. Here the point is Job's inability to *control,* following the line of the introductory questions.

God himself made Behemoth (vs. 15). He is one of the "works of God" and yet is utterly beyond man's control. He resists all attempts to capture him (vs. 24, although the margin of the Revised Standard Version is probably the correct rendering, the phrase "in his eyes" referring to a popular belief that the real hippopotamus was captured as his eyes were blinded with clay).

Can You Draw Out Leviathan? (41:1-34)

Once again the general features of the picture point to an actual animal, in this case the crocodile (see the descriptive phrases in vss. 13-17, 22-24, 30-32). But there can be no doubt that the poet used the crocodile to symbolize the ancient monster of "the deep" which always stood for the chaotic and demonic forces of the world (see Ps. 74:14 and Job 26:12). The full ironic force of the speech appears precisely in the fact that man is unable to deal with the crocodile, unable to domesticate it (vss. 3-9) or even to capture it (vss. 25-34); how much less is he able to control the vast forces of the universe about him, forces that defy his understanding and dwarf his strength!

Verses 10 and 11 make the application so far as Job's case is concerned. If man is not able to stand up to one such element of God's order, how can he stand up to God? Thus the priority of God in all matters is established. No one is able to anticipate God (vs. 11). Here the ground is cut finally from any view of God that places him at the end of man's thought or worship or activity. God is not one who can be placated or appeased. He remains forever the First Actor. He is not recipient, but Giver. He has his own questions to ask, his own gifts to give, his own righteousness to bestow.

Verse 12 is difficult and is, in fact, missing in the Greek translation. As it stands in the Revised Standard Version it does serve one useful purpose: to bring up again the subject of "Leviathan." From here on to the end of the chapter the poem is concerned with elaborating the picture of this beast. It is so elaborate, in fact, that one may suspect here some additions to the original, although if this be the case the balance between the actual and the mythical elements in the picture is still nicely preserved. Particularly apt expressions occur in verses 15, 28, 29, 30, 31, and 32. The association of "light," "sparks," and "smoke" (vss. 18-21) is often explained as a natural exaggeration of a description of a crocodile, or as poetic imagery. It is possible that the explanation, however, is to be found in the author's intent to suggest by this image the primeval creature of the sea, and by these very elements to stress the unnatural character of such a creature and its power.

The Second Response of Job (42:1-6)

Paralleling 40:3-5 there now appears a final word from Job. The Revised Standard Version clearly indicates by the use of single quotation marks that in his answer Job repeats the questions that have been asked of him (compare 42:3 with 38:2, and 42:4 with 38:3 and 40:7).

The answer begins with a confession, not of wrong, or even of wrong knowledge, but of God's power. The primary effect of God's speeches to Job has been to change the dimension or orientation of the problem. Heretofore Job has been concerned with himself and with the necessity to justify himself and his ways. Now he knows that God is sufficient for everything (so the Hebrew). One may say that the real change for Job is to have come to the place where God alone is important.

In this context Job can say of himself that he has spoken concerning things he neither understood nor was able to control. He *did* understand his own case. But on the narrow basis of that understanding he has wrongly launched an indictment of the totality of being and even of God. He can now accept the fact that God and his governance of man's life, and even his disposition of rewards and retribution, are ultimately beyond man's power to comprehend.

But there is still another element to Job's "confession." And this is the greatest, because the real power of the book does not lie in the realm of man's understanding but in the realm of his being. It is *Job* himself who matters, not his reason. The great conclusion of the book is Job's passage from a formal understanding of God—right or wrong—to a firsthand knowledge. Now his eye sees God. This is not to be equated with a kind of mystical experience, or even with another way of saying that now Job *knows more about* God. He does not; perhaps it would be truer to say he knows less about him. But he has come face to face with God as a Person. God is no longer an object to be discussed, a fact to be known, a truth to be comprehended. God is God. Nor is it exactly appropriate for us to assume that such a meeting left Job *at peace.* It left him first of all overwhelmed with the sense of his own incompleteness and his creatureliness in the presence of the Almighty (vs. 6; "despise" is not an exact rendering). It left him also ready to "repent in dust and ashes." Certainly it is not to be thought that this repentance was for sins such as the friends have formerly laid to his account. Neither is it enough to say that Job repented of his "pride." Rather, as the parallel to the first line of the verse shows, "repentance" is the mood of the creature man who realizes that he is creature, and that God is forever God.

Rather than vindication on his own terms, as Job has asked and confidently expected, he now has repentance. Vindication has come and will come, but it is not vindication by Job; it is God's gracious bestowal, the word of God which pronounces Job righteous and the grace that accepts him as such. Thus Job stands at the midpoint between the Garden of Eden and the New Testament assurance of justification by faith. Job is a titanic figure of sinful man—not sinner by the Law or against the Law but sinner challenging God and claiming to be divine. This sinner is still met by the God of grace who has called to him as he did to Adam, saying in effect, "Where are you?" (Gen. 3:9). And Job helps us see that it is in the mood of repentance that God's coming in his Word and his announcement of grace are to be received.

THE EPILOGUE
Job 42:7-17

The modern reader, accustomed to contemporary standards of artistic creation, may come to the Epilogue to the Book of Job with a feeling of surprise and even of disappointment that the dramatic power of the speeches of the Lord is given this somewhat prosy ending and that the point of the long argument seems to be lost in a return to the original situation.

Although the disappointment is not without its validity, there are some things that must be said in defense of the present ar-

rangement of the book. For one thing it can be remembered that
the author was using for his own purpose an ancient story, designed in its original form to illustrate genuine and disinterested
goodness. The story must have included approximately the very
ending we find in Job 42:7-17 and been used in its entirety by the
later author. As he had disregarded the details of the Prologue in
developing his argument, so the apparent discrepancies between
the argument and the Epilogue did not give him concern.

Again it must be emphasized that the story is not entirely out
of harmony with the argument of the complete book. The author
challenges and demolishes the belief that beween man's piety and
his prosperity, between his wickedness and his suffering, there
was a correspondence so evident that it could be used as a basis
for answering life's questions, but he does not anywhere, save in
Job's exaggerated and later discarded protests, affirm that there is
no connection. The existence of basic moral principles in the
order of history and human existence is once again stated in the
Epilogue.

The Epilogue also confirms what might be missed in the argument, namely, that Job, for all his errors and his exaggerations, is
nevertheless closer to the truth than the three friends. Job is the
one who has spoken "what is right" of God. Although this is not
to be taken as a blanket endorsement of all the words of Job, it
does point to greater error in the half-truths spoken by the
friends.

Finally there are touches in the Epilogue which illustrate beautifully the fact that a change has taken place in Job himself, and
which even hint at the meaning of that change. Job here is one
who has learned to receive. He accepts generosity even from the
friends, a token of his new reception of God's grace by which he
can be said to have been justified. Job thus prefigures the Christian man in his acceptance of grace as he has before illustrated
the deep need of all mankind for justification.